making business writing happen

Also available in this series:

making it happen

making business writing happen

A simple and effective guide to writing well

Ralph Brown

ALLEN&UNWIN

To Heather

First published in 2001 as *Making Business Writing Easy* by Media Associates
This edition published in 2003 by Allen & Unwin

Allen & Unwin
83 Alexander Street
Crows Nest NSW 2065
Australia
Phone: (61 2) 8425 0100
Fax: (61 2) 9906 2218
Email: info@allenandunwin.com
Web: www.allenandunwin.com

National Library of Australia
Cataloguing-in-Publication entry:

Brown, Ralph, 1949–
    Making business writing happen: a simple and effective
    guide to writing well.
    Rev. ed.
    Includes index.
    ISBN 1 86508 963 X.

    1. Business writing. 2. Communication in management.
    I. Brown, Ralph, 1949– Making business writing easy: what
    effective writers really do. II. Title. (Series: Making it happen)

808.066658

Layout by Coral Lee
Text design by Peta Nugent
Printed in Australia by McPherson's Printing Group

10 9 8 7 6 5 4 3 2 1

making it happen

Are you committed to changing things for the better? Are you searching for ways to make your organisation more effective? Are you trying to help your people and organisation to improve, but are seriously strapped for time and money? If you are, then this Making It Happen book is written specifically for you.

Every book in the series is designed to assist change agents to get things done ... to make new programs really happen ... without costing the organisation an arm and a leg and without taking up all of your valuable time.

Each book in the series is written by a top consultant in the field who does not simply theorise about their subject of expertise but who explains specifically how to implement a program that will really work for your work unit or organisation. Vital advice on what works and what doesn't work, what tricks to use and traps to avoid, plus suggested strategies for implementation, templates and material to photocopy, and checklists to gauge your readiness — each book in the series is filled with useful information, all written in clear, practical language that enables you to make things happen, fast.

Help your people and work unit to increase their performance and love their work through implementing a program from the Making It Happen series and reap the rewards that successful change agents deserve.

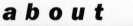

about
the book

'Please find enclosed our brochure for your perusal ...'
'With reference to your letter of ...'
'Please do not hesitate to contact the writer ...'

Tired of writing formal business letters using the same old clichés? Rather than giving your writing more credibility, formal conventions make business writing unnecessarily complicated and impersonal. And what's more, many of those conventions are becoming increasingly redundant as business focuses more on effective communication and building relationships.

So how can you write more effectively? This book tells you what you *really* need to know to become an effective writer. You won't find any references to correct use of the auxiliary verb, or the intervening prepositional phrase—just simple, practical ideas that you will use and remember.

In *Making Business Writing Happen* you'll learn how to apply the 'golden rule of all communication' and the 'five keys to effective writing' to transform stuffy, ambiguous and obscure writing into letters, reports and proposals that anyone could read and absorb — first time around.

But as with most skills, reading about them is not enough. Take advantage of the activities, samples and checklists in the final chapter to put the ideas into action and start writing more effectively today!

about the author

Ralph Brown teaches business writing and related topics in workshops throughout New Zealand and in Australia. He has a passion for helping adults discover their potential as writers. His career includes 17 years in business and a similar time in writing, reporting and directing for television in New Zealand and on secondment to the BBC. He holds a degree in psychology and a post-graduate diploma in journalism. Brown is managing director of Media Associates, based in Christchurch, New Zealand.

acknowledgements

In the past, I've edited books and, in the process, persuaded myself that good books are a team effort. Oddly enough, now that I'm the writer, I'm even more sure that it's true.

I'd like to thank my brother Michael for his part in our long-running, enjoyable, productive and creative working relationship, and for his comments on the drafts and his extensive contribution to the layout.

Thanks, too, to Alan Loney, Sue Neale Brown and my wife Heather for their detailed assessments of the drafts and their suggestions and encouragement.

Thanks to all those who've taken part in my business writing workshops and shared their curiosities, uncertainties and passions, and helped me refine what really matters to its simplest form.

contents

introduction

This book is especially for people who write business letters and reports, so most of the examples are from business. But think of it as a resource to develop your writing and language skills generally. You can use many of the techniques in presentations, in meetings and even in conversation.

NOT JUST WRITING, NOT JUST BUSINESS

You'll discover how easy it is to use the power of the English language and how conventions have made business writing unnecessarily complicated, and robbed it of its humanity. The conventions made sense centuries ago but many of them don't now, and they are disappearing as business focuses on effective communication and building relationships. Even technology is helping the process along.

The principles of effective writing are the same, whether you are writing a business letter or report, a personal letter, novel, letter to the editor, television script, article for a community newspaper or even a note on a card.

MAKING IT HAPPEN

It's almost certainly going to be much easier than you think.

Many people tell me they want to learn the rules of formal business writing. They assume that they need to study the rules of grammar and formal phrasing that so called knowledgeable writers use in business letters.

Imagine how dry, boring and complicated that would be. It would also be a waste of time because our real interest is in being effective. It's best to think of formal business writing, what some people like to call Commercial English, as a convention. It's not a set of rules, because rules would suggest that they exist for logical reasons or that there is some authority behind them.

As we will see, there isn't.

Grammar is a little different. There are rules of grammar, but your experience as a speaker of English gives you most of them. You can avoid breaking many of them by writing in a simple, conversational style. You might have to check a grammar book occasionally, but some of the conventions of grammar are arbitrary and we can ignore them without offending or distracting anyone — except people who like to let us know how much they know.

The alternative to learning grammar and the conventions is simpler, more useful and more fun. It will not only change your writing, it will help you whenever you use language.

Here's what we need to do first. Ask yourself this question: What do I really want to achieve by becoming an effective writer?

To get you started, here's what most people tell me:

'I want people to read what I write — all the way through.'
'I want to persuade people.'
'I want to build relationships with my readers. I want to build relationships with my audiences.'
'I want to be more precise.'
'I want people to take notice. I want to have an impact.'

The words vary, but their essence is, 'I want to be more effective'. So let's concentrate on making you a more effective communicator.

To be frank, most people write letters that are impersonal, lifeless and cold. They begin letters with lines like, 'With reference to our telephone conversation with you on March 28 ...' They're not cold people, they just write that way. They can show a real interest in you when they talk to you on the telephone, then send you a confirming letter in formal, stock phrases that say, 'You're no one special'. It's not good writing and in business it's not good service. Most of the average writers I've met are not content with their writing but they are not sure what to do about it.

THE REAL DIFFERENCES

After more than twenty-five years of examining my own professional writing, and the work of journalists, presenters, orators, business leaders and employees of businesses, government departments and local authorities, I've decided that all you need to bridge the gap between average and effective are five qualities of writing.

Let's call them the five keys to effective writing: *simple, informal, direct, active* and *personal*. If you want an acronym, it's SIDAP. You're going to find them easy to learn and apply.

Chapter 1

Six ways to transform your writing

- Maximising skills you already have

- The golden rule of all communication

- The five keys to effective writing

- Putting the five keys to work

- An easy way to edit your writing

Here's something really odd. It's tempting to say that most average writers are ineffective because they don't know how to communicate on paper. In fact, it's as if they *do* know but strive to do the opposite. They have been misled by the people who keep the myths of business writing alive.

■ MAXIMISING SKILLS YOU ALREADY HAVE

All you have to do is get to know the five keys and use them. To make it simpler, they overlap. Use one and you'll often find that you're using at least one other. *Simple, informal, direct, active* and *personal* — they're natural companions.

You can use them as a tool to edit your work. They will help whenever you are not satisfied with a sentence or paragraph and you want to work out what to do about it.

DEVELOPING YOUR EAR

If it doesn't sound right when you read it aloud, change the phrase or sentence until it does. Develop your ear for language by reading your work aloud routinely, especially to a willing colleague or partner.

When I was a television reporter it was routine to read a script aloud, make changes, make more when we edited the pictures and more still when we recorded it in the sound booth. There was rarely time to retype and some of my scripts were such a mess that I often just adlibbed around all the corrections. The sound was the real test.

You might be thinking that letters, reports and memos shouldn't be written for reading aloud, that written communication is, well, different. Quite right. It is different. When we write we have the chance to polish every phrase if we want to. But that polish should be the main difference between business writing and business conversation.

> **The only difference between business writing and business conversation should be the polish.**

MAKING JUDGEMENTS

Your ear for language combined with the five keys to effective writing will help you decide whether a particular line or paragraph works. You'll be making judgements even as the words begin to form in your mind.

Don't be put off by the thought that making judgements about writing is a bit out of your league because you haven't trained as a critic of English usage. In fact, you have. You certainly know when something sounds odd or when language is used inappropriately. Take a couple of those examples that circulate on the Internet:

'Our wines leave you nothing to hope for.' — Menu in Swiss restaurant

'The Manager has personally passed all the water served here.' — In a hotel in Acapulco

If you are a native speaker of English, you'll know that both those sentences have other meanings. It's a very complex language full of double meanings, subtlety and sometimes absurd idiom. When you are in a conversation the right words for the message, the occasion and the relationship just pop into your head as you need them — usually anyway. What an amazing skill! We'll be building on it in five specific ways. But first, there's something we need to establish.

■ THE GOLDEN RULE OF ALL COMMUNICATION

If we want our readers to read and remember, if we want them to sit up, concentrate and go away with lasting memories, we have to be passionate about the golden rule of all communication.

The golden rule of all communication: be audience-centred.

Focus on what your readers want to know, their background knowledge, their interest in the topic, their relationship with you and anything else about them that will help to make your communication effective. It's just what you would do in business conversation or at a party, yet most people write for *themselves*. They deny it, but they do. They cram in everything they want to say and assume that their readers or audience are just as interested in the content as they are.

Putting your reader or your audience first won't stop you saying what you need to say, it will just make you more effective.

We have a saying around our office: 'It's not what you tell them that counts. It's what they remember.' They'll remember if you make it relevant, interesting, credible and intelligible. Focus on your readers and use the five keys to effective writing.

It's not what you tell them that counts. It's what they remember.

Put yourself in an audience-centred frame of mind whenever you write. Without that frame of mind, you cannot be effective.

People say it's easy enough to be audience-centred if they are writing to one person, but they might be writing to thousands of people at a time. Yes, it is a complication, but a minor one. You might need to generalise about the audience but that is not difficult to do, and it's certainly much better than writing with no thought for your readers.

If you think that some of your audience might be more interested in your topic than others, write for those who are specially interested and try to drag in as many other readers as you can by supplying essential background and coming up with surprises that will motivate even a less interested reader to continue reading. Journalists do it every day.

■ THE FIVE KEYS TO EFFECTIVE WRITING

I know you might well be tempted to skip our first key because it's obvious. It's the old KISS principle, right? Stay with me. It's the first of our five keys to effective writing and the one everyone expects, but keeping it simple is a little more complicated than it might appear — just a little. And it's important.

KEY 1. SIMPLE

Let's agree first that expressing what we need to say with fewer words is a virtue. It's easy to say, but most writers have phrases they use regularly and have never thought about changing. See if you recognise any of these:

LONG	SHORT
exact opposites	opposites
rather unique	unique
specific example	example
in six months' time	in six months

You get the picture. Don't bother memorising them, just make sure you eliminate unnecessary words.

Stand back

Now, here's the slight complication. Sometimes taking words out won't help you. But being audience-centred will. Just stand back and ask yourself what your readers really need to know to understand your point.

Let's take an example. A city council sends out regular notices with this long-winded sentence at the top: 'If you are not the owner of this property but are a tenant it would be appreciated if you would pass this leaflet on to the owner for their information.' A headline, 'To the owner' would have done it, because that's all the reader needs to know. Usually, just finding a substitute for a complicated word or phrase is all you need. But not always.

A: What's another word for differentiation?
B: What's the context?

A: We need more product differentiation to compete in the home construction market.

B: Why do you want to tell them that we need more product differentiation?

A: Well, because I want to show our customers that our houses offer them more.

B: So, we need to show our customers that our houses have more benefits?

A: I guess so.

B: Just say that.

A: Oh, yes ... Thanks.

Asking yourself 'Would my reader understand? What does my reader need to know?' often saves you the time of consulting someone else or using your thesaurus, and gives you a much better result than just changing a word. Notice that these questions will help you use the golden rule of all communication — be audience-centred.

You can ask yourself the same questions with phrases too, especially many of those tired ones we use out of habit. Stand back and ask 'What does the reader need to know to understand my point?'

WHAT PEOPLE OFTEN WRITE	WHEN THEY REALLY MEAN ...
as far as we are concerned	we believe
despite the fact that	although
the volume of demand	the demand
the level of wages rose	wages rose
do a study of the effects of	study, research

Sometimes *more* words

Sometimes *more* words can make writing much simpler. Take jargon. For example: 'Our terms are f.o.b. to L.A.F.T.A. customers'.

It might be intelligible to first-time exporters with more words: 'Our terms for customers from the Latin America Free Trade Association member countries are for us to pay all costs of transport, loading charges and insurance to our ports. You would be responsible for all costs once the goods are on the ship.'

Here's the key point: use simple words and ideas, even if you need more words. Ask yourself 'Are those words really working for the reader?' If not, delete them or find a simpler way. Of course, if your reader happens to be an experienced exporter, the jargon in the example might well be simpler.

You'll save yourself words and the reader will appreciate the conciseness of your letter. The principle remains.

Use simple words and ideas, even if you need *more* words.

Use a simpler construction

Simple sentences do our readers a favour and avoid many grammatical problems.

> *'I will send you my report.'*
> *'The office will be closed on Thursday.'*

A simple construction gives you clarity, but a string of sentences made up of short, simple statements could make you seem simple yourself, or curt, so it makes sense to join some compatible sentences together. You'll also achieve a more natural and interesting rhythm; but do make sure they're compatible.

> *'Call me as soon as it arrives and I will ask someone to collect it.'*
> *'Thanks for the offer but I will be out of town that day.'*

Some sentences put the reader on hold. It's as if the writer is saying, 'I'm going to tell you something, but just before I do, I want to give you some background'.

> *'Being a double agent, she risked her life in both countries.'*

'Being a double agent,' makes no sense on its own, but provides some background for the real point, that she risked her life in both countries. *Having, seeing, considering* and many other words ending in 'ing' will create the same effect if you use them to start a sentence. *Due to, owing to* and *although* will do it too.

> *'Although it is the second time you have reported that your rates payment was lost in the mail, we have decided not to add the penalty payment.'*

So are these more complicated sentences that put the reader on hold good or bad? It depends how well you construct them. If you keep the first part of your sentence (the bit before the comma) short, you could give your writing some valuable variety. Used without thought, such sentences put readers on hold for too long, and they begin to wonder whether it's time for coffee or whose dog is barking in the distance.

PUTTING YOUR READER 'ON HOLD'	SIMPLE ALTERNATIVES
Being a company that prides itself on the service it has provided to the residents of this community over two generations, we would attend to your order immediately.	We pride ourselves on our service and would attend to your order immediately.

Having taken so long to research and write the report and check that it addresses all the issues that the Managing Director listed in the briefing just before Christmas, I am now worried that everyone will have lost interest.	I have taken two months to write the report and I am now worried that everyone will have lost interest.
For the purposes of obtaining a permit and bearing in mind the significance of a delay should our first application be refused, we have decided to prepare a detailed plan.	We have decided to prepare a detailed plan to ensure that we obtain a permit on our first application.

If you are going to put your reader on hold, it's especially important to make sure that the sentence sounds natural when you read it aloud.

> 'Tramping in the mountains, we came across an injured hunter and Gillian called Search and Rescue on her cell phone.'

Starting with 'Tramping in the mountains …' seems awkward. It's much more natural to say: 'While we were tramping in the mountains, we came across an injured hunter and Gillian called Search and Rescue on her cell phone.'

KEY 2. INFORMAL
Let's get controversial.

If you were taught that there's an approved formal way of writing for business, you were misled. Your boss or colleagues are wrong if they tell you that a business letter must contain such sentences and phrases as:

> Enclosed please find … for your perusal.
> I refer to your letter of March 16 …
> Thank you for your letter of 14th inst.
> Your letter of April 3 refers and we confirm …
> We are in receipt of your letter of September 5 and wish to advise that …
> … assuring you of our best attention at all times …
> If you have any questions please do not hesitate to contact the writer.

Imagine that you call a computer company and have a perfectly normal conversation with the sales rep. Then two days later you receive a letter beginning, 'With reference to our telephone conversation of August 7 …'

We wouldn't dream of finishing a conversation by saying, 'If you have any questions please contact the speaker'. Why shouldn't we write, 'Please call me on my direct line if you have any questions', or something similarly informal?

What to tell people in the office

Most people write formally because teachers and bosses have told them that it's the 'proper' way to write. You need something to show they're wrong to think that such stuffy writing has official approval.

Let's bring out the gurus of English usage.

Henry Fowler wrote *A Dictionary of Modern English Usage,* which has since been revised by Sir Ernest Gowers, reprinted many times and distributed throughout the English-speaking world. If you want authoritative support on a point of English usage, consult Fowler. Fowler calls stuffy, formal business writing commercialese. I think we can safely say that he doesn't approve:

> *'... much of it originated in a wish to treat the customer with almost obsequious respect. But it has become an artificial jargon ...'* — H.W. Fowler, *Fowler's Modern English Usage*

If you think that the others in your office will still say, 'Yes, but it's the way we were taught', tell them their teachers were wrong. Quote this to them and tell them who wrote it — and when.

> *'We have no hesitation in reporting that Commercial English is not only objectionable to all those who have the purity of the language at heart but also contrary to the true interests of commercial life, sapping its vitality and encouraging the use of dry, meaningless formulae just where vigorous and arresting English is the chief requisite.'* — The Departmental Committee on the Teaching of English in England (1921)

Who would have more authority to decide what is proper or approved in the teaching of the English language? You could say with confidence that the idea of a separate formal language for business writing was officially condemned in 1921. It didn't stop many teachers and employers insisting on it, but they had no authority to do so.

I find the argument compelling, but I remember a young woman in a workshop who was certainly not convinced.

'So you are telling us that we should follow the advice of some people who were writing in 1921?'

'Yes.'

'Well, that's ridiculous! Things are totally different now.' The others were amused, and waiting.

'You're right of course. Business and writing have both changed since then. But would you say that business culture and business conversations have become more formal or informal since then?'

'Informal. So why does it matter what they said in 1921?'

'Because it shows that Commercial English is an antiquated convention. It's not just a little bit old-fashioned or a slightly conservative way of writing. If it was time to let it go in 1921, it's even more true now.' Her expression gave nothing away but by the end of the day she was writing informally and pleased with the result.

Spread the word. Formal language is not 'correct'. It's just stuffy. Forget the dry, meaningless formulae. Join the crusade. Let's communicate.

Don't address the nation

There's another reason many people write formally.

They think they are addressing the nation. They imagine that the communication is too important for plain speaking, so they use formal language in the vain hope that they and the message will have a special authority.

Formal language can work but only for a very narrow range of situations. It can work for orators:

> *'My fellow Americans, ask not what your country can do for you. Ask what you can do for your country. My fellow citizens of the world, ask not what America can do for you, but what together we can do for the freedom of man.'*
> — President John F. Kennedy at his inauguration

Imagine this. You have just been appointed chief executive of your organisation so you call the staff together and tell them, 'My fellow employees, ask not what your company can do for you. Ask what you can do for your company.' I think you'll agree that it would not be a winning line. What's the difference?

If you were not in President Kennedy's audience that day, imagine it now. You are surrounded by hundreds of thousands of people at a turning point in history. Before you, perhaps in the distance, is not just a new president, but a president with a very different style. A dramatic moment?

Here's the key difference that can make formal writing appropriate. For President Kennedy's inauguration the drama was in the minds of the audience. If you are the new chief executive, you might have a sense of drama because it's your first day and you are a little nervous talking to all the staff, but for them it's just another day.

It's easy to misread the drama of the occasion. If your first draft is cold, complex and sounds unnatural, maybe it's because you haven't looked at the drama from the audience's point of view. Try reading this extract aloud:

*After initial periods of discussion the attendees were questioned to elicit
their acceptance of the organisational changes required. We found a negative
correlation between the time of initial discussion and acceptance of the
proposed changes.*

Pompous, isn't it? Let's try a more informal approach.

*We gave each group time to get to know each other and our plans to change
the organisation. Then we asked for their opinions. We found that the more
time we let them spend together, the less they liked our proposal.*

Oh, that's what they were saying! Were they trying to hide the meaning with complex words and ideas so that we wouldn't discover that everyone hated their proposal? See in the redraft how appropriate informality also makes writing simpler.

Signs often tell you that writers believe they are addressing the nation. I found this one at Christchurch international airport.

ATTENTION:

Parents or guardians are required to keep children well clear
of the baggage conveyor. Injuries can occur to fingers or hands
when the conveyor belt is operating. Thank you.

Notice the formality of 'Parents or guardians are required ...' and 'Injuries can occur ...' It's both formal and long-winded. We can make it less formal and more effective.

DANGER:

The baggage conveyors can injure small fingers.
Please keep children well clear.

Most people prefer you to talk to them on paper. Your writing inevitably becomes more informal when you move into conversational mode. Resist the temptation to add pompous, formal language you'd be embarrassed to use in a conversation with your reader. You can even write technical reports that talk to the reader. Notice how much more people read and remember when you do!

Laying it on the line — informally

Many people like the idea of informality but they are sure it wouldn't apply to their business writing. Usually they have something to do with enforcing the law or they need to be aware that their letters might end up in court as Exhibit 1. It's important work and they can't risk any misinterpretation. It's usually not too difficult to persuade them that they can be more precise by writing more informally and in a more audience-centred way.

Let's take an example of a council employee writing to a resident. I have shortened it slightly.

Dear Madam

ILLEGAL REFUSE DUMPING

This officer has obtained an article from a pile of refuse illegally dumped in High Street. The article had been directed to yourself, indicating that you have been in possession of the article. It is an offence to dump refuse in or on any public place, or in the case of private land, in or on that private land without the consent of its occupier.

It is also an offence to leave refuse, once deposited, in or on any public place, or in or on any private land without the consent of its occupier.

Any person found to have committed an offence under the Litter Act 1979 can be liable for a fine of up to $750.00 or, in the case of a body corporate, $5000.00.

The refuse must be removed from its current location and disposed of at the landfill within four days from the date of this letter.

Yours faithfully

He's really letting her know that she has broken the law, but it's full of official-sounding formality — much of it irrelevant to the careless woman who dropped her rubbish bag. Usually, official-sounding formality doesn't make our writing seem more important, just pompous and often complicated.

Here's a less formal, but still very firm, alternative.

Dear Mrs Jones

ILLEGAL REFUSE DUMPING

Council staff have found a rubbish bag in High Street containing mail addressed to you. I must assume that it is yours.

It is an offence to dump rubbish in any public place and if we have to prosecute, you could be fined up to $750.

The bag is near the fountain. Please remove it immediately.

Yours sincerely

This time we have called her Mrs Jones, we didn't quote from the Litter Act of 1979 or include references to bodies corporate. We have still told her what we want done and what the consequences might be if it is not done. If it goes to court, the judge will know that we have warned her in terms anyone could understand.

How informal should I be?

Make sure it's *appropriate* informality.

So what's appropriate?

It's appropriate to the reader and your relationship, just as it would be in conversation. Now that you are an audience-centred writer, you'll be thinking constantly about your reader and the degree of informality they would find appropriate.

Imagine this: you don't see the head of your organisation more than about once a month, but you have a cordial relationship. You are on first name terms and once had a hilarious discussion with her about raising teenagers. She has just sent you a fax praising your work, but it has come at an awkward time.

Your first draft begins like this:

Dear Judith

Ugh! This is Judith you are writing to. Detached, formal.

I was encouraged by your facsimile on September 20 and pleased to discover that your commendation has been recorded on my personal file.

Elegant 19th-century writing but too stuffy for 21st-century readers.

Even so, I must raise an issue made more delicate by your appreciative comments.

Long formal sentence with long formal words.

I have recently been approached by Sloan and Company to undertake employment with them in a more senior position than would be available to me within Acme in the foreseeable future and have made an irrevocable decision to relinquish my position as your Customer Services Officer at your earliest convenience ...

A letter like that is going to make her wonder whether you are such an asset after all. A more relaxed approach will give you something more appropriate to the warm relationship.

	Dear Judith
More like conversation. Notice there's no date.	Thanks for the fax. I really appreciated your comments.
A light bridge between *thanks* and *I quit*.	In fact, they leave me a little embarrassed.
Less formal. Shorter words.	I've just accepted a senior position with Sloan and Company and need to leave Acme by the end of the month ...

Most people believe they are keeping safe by sending out a formal letter, but the standard formal letter erodes your relationship, especially if it tells your reader that you are not especially interested.

	Dear Mrs Carter
Mrs Carter wonders: 'Is this really the nice young woman I spoke to?' Formal and stuffy.	Further to our telephone conversation with you on June 21, I have pleasure in supplying our brochure for your perusal.
Unnecessary, formal, even obsequious.	We trust that this action meets with your approval.
Stuffy, but at least it fits the routine tone of the letter.	If you require any further information, please do not hesitate to contact the writer.
Too formal for a letter to a named reader.	Yours faithfully

It's very ordinary. By using clichés, writers imply that your enquiry was nothing special — so you are getting the routine letter. It is certainly not the way Sue Wilson would have spoken to Mrs Carter on the telephone. Try reading it aloud.

She could have written back to Mrs Carter this way:

	Dear Mrs Carter
Note: 'Thanks' not 'Further to'. Mentioning the motorcycles says she remembers the conversation. It is no longer a routine letter.	Thanks for the conversation on the telephone on Monday and your interest in more information about our range of motorcycles.

She even remembers the model.	I have marked the pages in the brochure showing the 500cc model we talked about.
More likely to build the relationship than, 'please do not hesitate to contact the writer'.	There's a new shipment due in about a month. I would like to call you then, but in the meantime, please let me know if there's anything else you need.
'Sincerely' because she has named Mrs Carter in the salutation.	Sincerely

I hope you will agree that it would be appropriately informal for a letter that follows a warm conversation on the telephone. Do you also agree that it is more friendly and better service than the formal clichés in the first letter?

If you disagree with parts of it, you are making different judgements. You are perhaps interpreting the relationship that developed in the conversation on the telephone slightly differently. You might prefer 'Thank you' to 'Thanks' regardless of the relationship. We don't have to agree on everything.

Informality and speeches

Informality is essential for all speeches, except when you really are addressing the nation at a time of crisis or being inaugurated as the next president of the United States.

As you write your speech or presentation, imagine yourself saying it to just two people, and talk to them. Be as informal as you would when talking to two people at work. They don't see themselves as a crowd, but as individuals.

Contract your words in the script — don't rely on making the contractions as you speak. So make liberal (but not contrived) use of *you're, we're, I've, they've, don't, haven't*. It's essential. Incidentally, be careful with the sound of your contractions. *They're not*, for instance, sounds much better than *they aren't*.

All the ideas in this book can be applied to speeches and presentations, whether you write them or not. Appropriate informality is a vital beginning.

KEY 3. DIRECT

We say we want people to tell us what they mean, but we don't always deliver directness ourselves. I once suggested to an accountant who wrote monthly reports for the board of a large company that he should come right out with it.

'Do you mean make a recommendation?'

'Yes.'

'Isn't that a bit risky? The board might not like it.'

'Isn't that what they want you to do?'

'Well true, but I can do it more safely if I just describe the issues.'

Yes it's safe, but it's not effective writing to hide your meaning. It's not good service either. Some people say that it's not their job to recommend, only to advise, but they can still get to the point. Ask yourself, what is my real point here?

In writing, being direct means two things:

- Coming right out with it.
- Being specific.

Watch out for signs!

Watch how people who write signs dress simple ideas up into something more formal and less direct. Take the signs on lifts. The usual one is:

In event of fire do not use lifts

A hotel in Sydney puts it this way:

In case of fire do not use lifts

Are they suggesting that it is too risky to use the lifts; that we could cause a fire by just getting into a lift? A grand hotel took it to a new level:

Do not use lifts in case of fire

Now that's daft. What they all mean is 'Don't use the lifts in a fire' or 'Never use lifts in a fire' or, perhaps, 'If there is a fire, use the stairs'. It's as if they believe that direct language wouldn't convey the importance of their message, yet their indirectness seems pompous and hides the meaning. Direct language might save more lives.

Here's one from a council.

CAUTION
Track closed due to unsafe conditions

Does that mean that once the weather clears it will be safe? Does caution suggest that we can use it at our own risk but the council suggests we be cautious? It's a real example. I was there. What the council should have pointed out was that the steps just a couple of metres below had collapsed and if I had taken even a few more steps I would have plunged over a cliff and onto rocks. A more direct alternative would be:

DANGER
Track collapsed. Keep away!

You will see indirect language in business writing everywhere. Often, it's not audience-centred and more focus on the reader's interests would allow the writer to bring out the real meaning. Take this extract from a brochure for a company of consultant engineers:

All design work is undertaken as a team at a single location, hence leading to an efficient flow of information, a high degree of innovation and mutual problem solving and a minimum wastage of human resource.

Why should we care? It's not audience-centred and it's not direct. We expect a brochure to tell us what the company can do for us. Why did they hide their meaning? Perhaps they really meant:

We can solve your engineering problems very efficiently. We have one design team, and because we are all in the same office, we're able to exchange information and ideas easily.

It sometimes takes more courage, but you can be more economical, authoritative and persuasive if you come right out with it. Even so, let's acknowledge that we often want to soften our message to be tactful, just as we would in speech, but that's being audience-centred so it still counts as effective writing.

Being specific and coming right out with it can have the same meaning, but let *being specific* remind you to add detail where it's relevant to the audience. It can lend authority and interest to your writing to mention how many people came to the meeting, the number of people in the queue when you were kept waiting at the bank or that Janet brought red carnations for the reception desk this morning and they came from her own garden.

KEY 4. ACTIVE

Why does this famous extract work so well?

> *'We shall fight on the beaches.*
> *We shall fight on the landing grounds.*
> *We shall fight in the fields and in the streets.*
> *We shall fight in the hills.*
> *We shall never surrender.'* — Sir Winston Churchill

The whole speech succeeds for many reasons, including the repetition, the rhythm and the word *shall,* which indicates determination. But our real interest here is in active language. If you are in any doubt about what I mean by active, ask yourself: Is there any doubt who will be fighting on the beaches or on the landing grounds? Active language tells you who is responsible for the action. It gives your writing authority, adds interest and it's more appealing to read or hear.

Would the British nation have been as inspired if Churchill had said:

> *The beaches will be fought on.*
> *The landing grounds will be fought on.*
> *So will the fields and the streets ...*

That's the passive version. Active speech makes it clear what is being done and who is doing it. There's a simple formula for active sentences:

Active = Actor + Verb (in that order)

An actor makes you think of a person, but keep in mind that you can have active sentences if the actor is, say, an organisation or a dog, as long as there is an action and it's clear who, or what, did it.

Note that the actor comes first. 'The report was read by Jane' has both an actor plus a verb, but 'Jane read the report' puts them in the right order. Doesn't it sound stronger too?

Don't be distracted by the form of the verb. *We fight, we shall not fight* and *we fought* qualify as much as Churchill's 'We shall fight ...'

Active writing is not just some academic point of English usage. The difference is dramatic. Yet for some reason most business writers use passive language more often.

Can you identify the active and passive sentences in these pairs? Which do you prefer? The best test is to read them aloud.

A	B
Monitoring of customer satisfaction with the service was carried out by the sales staff.	The sales staff monitored our customers' satisfaction with the service.
Since the company's decision to proceed with the project several discussions have been held with interested parties.	Since the company decided to proceed we have discussed the project with interested parties.
A financial reporting system has been set up.	The company has set up a financial reporting system.
A quotation will be supplied by the end of the week.	We will send you a quotation by the end of the week.
A branch of Computer Corporation has just been opened in your street.	Computer Corporation has just opened a branch in your street.

Did you prefer the sentences in Column B? They are the active sentences. If you preferred one or two in Column A, just be sure that you recognise them as passive.

Yes, there is a place for passive language. Use it when you don't want to assign blame or responsibility. In your business you might want to write a memo calling attention to the fact that someone used the office car this morning without going through the reservation system. Others have done it before and you don't want it to happen again. You might decide that it's more constructive not to assign blame, so you have a choice.

You could use an active sentence with an anonymous actor as in 'Someone used the car this morning without booking it first'. It sounds ominous, as if you will be tracking the offender down before long, but it does rivet attention by being active. The passive alternative would be, 'The car was used this morning without being booked first'. Not exactly gripping, but the emphasis is now on the offence rather than the offender.

Occasionally, you will use a passive sentence for variety or to soften a sentence that might otherwise sound harsh or aggressive. Sometimes passive is more appropriate because the event is more important than the actor. For example, 'The President has been shot' works better than 'An unknown assassin has shot the President'.

Select vigorous verbs

Not all verbs were created equal. Strong verbs build more dramatic pictures.

WEAK VERBS	STRONGER VERBS
We *received* the cheque.	Your cheque *arrived* today.
We have *obtained* a report.	We have *commissioned* a report.
The board *considered* your submission.	The board *debated/discussed* your submission.

Some verbs are especially strong:

> *We* demanded *an apology.*
> *We* dispute *your claim.*
> *The court has* dismissed *your appeal.*

Untrained writers often work hard to find colourful or clever sounding adjectives to give their sentences more impact. Go for stronger verbs instead.

Sometimes verbs are so weak that nouns take over the sentence. The result is boring officialese.

STARRING BORING NOUNS (Notice the weak verbs)	STARRING VIGOROUS VERBS
The company gave *consideration* to your proposal.	The company *considered* your proposal.
The committee made *a recommendation* that you apply again next year.	The committee *recommended* that you apply again next year.
The scientists will conduct *an analysis* of the data.	The scientists *will analyse* the data.

The real power in writing comes from verbs. That's why effective writers prefer active language. It's more interesting, easier to absorb and more memorable. Decide that from now on you are an active writer who favours strong verbs.

KEY 5. PERSONAL

This is the big one.

I promised that the five keys to effective writing would be simple to use and, even better, that they would overlap. I said that if you use one, you'll find that you're using at least one other because they're natural companions.

There is no more natural companion to any of the other four than our final key: *personal*. Getting personal means including people, especially your reader or audience. When you get personal, your writing usually becomes more active and informal, it's often simpler and sometimes more direct. It is a very powerful technique, yet most writers strive to keep people out of their writing. Why? They are missing the opportunity to involve their readers or audiences, and it makes a very big difference.

Here's an extract from a community newsletter:

It is expected that a summary of the submissions on the city plan will be available at the beginning of May. The summary will be able to be inspected at the main office or public libraries.

Did you notice 'It is expected ...' and 'The summary will be able to be inspected ...'? Dull stuff. Someone has worked hard to keep the people out of that one. Let's put them in and focus on the reader.

We expect to have a summary of the submissions on the city plan ready by the beginning of May. You will be able to look through it at the main office, or your nearest library.

Did you notice *we, you, your*? Was it easier to read? Notice that in getting personal I also made it more informal and direct.

Remember the golden rule of all communication — be audience-centred. There's no easier way to put it to work for you than getting personal.

Many writers seem to assume that adding people makes their subject less important. It's as if they need to tell their audience, 'This is an important subject from an important organisation'. Too important for people? If the subject is important, it's only because of its relevance to people. If their organisations are important, it's only because of what they do for people.

Effective writers believe with a passion that it's the human element that makes writing important. It doesn't lower an organisation's status, it enhances it. By getting personal you will show that you and your organisation are good to deal with.

Most people find that words such as *you, I, we, your* and *our* make writing easier to read, more precise, more interesting, warmer and more memorable. You can take most dull letters, reports, memos and speeches and transform them by getting personal.

My favourite example of impersonal writing comes from a newsletter published by a government department:

> *Meetings and submissions have identified some issues that are considered not to have been given sufficient emphasis in the strategy.*

See, they managed to get all the people out of it!

The audience-pulling power of human interest

Most people are motivated by human interest. What people do, say and believe is usually far more interesting to most readers than information about objects, procedures, or reports of events that don't mention people. It's a powerful motivating tool to show how people are, were or could be involved. And remember that there is no human more interesting to the reader than the reader.

Let me give you an example. When I lived in the city, I used to write a newsletter for my neighbourhood support group. I tried to make it gossipy — in the best possible sense.

Everyone knows that most people like to read about themselves and their neighbours, but I realised just how much one day when I asked a couple of our co-ordinators to come up with some ideas for the newsletter. They said they would ring around the neighbours and suggested I call at their house at 7.30 that night. I turned up to find most of the street crowded into their lounge. They all had contributions to make. One told us about checking on a prowler, only to discover that it was his elderly neighbour stuck halfway through a window. She was in the room too and laughingly explained that she had lost her key and had decided to break in. Another's teenage son had just won a national yachting event. Another announced that his pig (I swear it's true) had a habit of getting loose and he would appreciate a call if anyone saw it out again.

It was absurd really. They were telling me, and everyone else, stories about themselves and their neighbours, which I would write up and distribute so that they could read them all over again. I did, and the feedback was great. They wanted more!

If you are in any doubt about the motivating power of human interest, consider the television programs you watch. Take, for instance, a television news item on an apparently dry topic, say, 'Rising exports lead to an improvement in the balance of payments'. You can be sure that television reporters won't just give you figures and factories. They would be far more likely to go to a factory first and show people, possibly just one or two people, as an example. The script might go something like this:

REPORTER: Joe McKenzie has known hard times. In the six years he's been with

Smith Manufacturing he's sometimes wondered whether there would even be a job to come back to the next week. It's very different now.

JOE: 'It's been great since the company got into exports. Yeah, there's heaps of work. Like, me and Charlie here make the casings and we're working 60 hours a week now just to keep up.'

REPORTER: Smith Manufacturing is typical of the companies that have contributed to the strong growth in exports. This company has succeeded in Poland and Italy. Others have won new or larger sales throughout Europe. It's where the growth has come this year and where it's expected to be for at least the next decade.

Make sure you harness the same audience-pulling power.

Most people find it easier to understand and remember new information if you can help them build a picture with people in it. Even technical reports have some human purpose, so show the effects on people. Tell your reader who did the tests, who made the decision, who is giving the advice, whose opinion you are reporting.

Ways of getting personal

First, get oriented. Think about your readers or audience. Never let them out of your mind. Write for them. Help them to understand, show them what's significant, interesting and relevant. Don't just give them the facts, show them why those facts are relevant. If they're not relevant to your reader, explain their relevance to other people. Virtually everything you will write about has some human relevance or purpose. Make the link and you will motivate your readers to read, understand and remember.

Start your paragraphs with a personal element, especially the word *you*. If you are editing, starting with *you* or *we* will almost always unravel a complex first draft. Watch though for predictability. If you start every paragraph with *you* or *I*, you'll lose your reader quickly. Occasionally, for variety, you might want to add an impersonal sentence, but avoid those standard, lofty, impersonal phrases: 'It can be seen that ... It will be appreciated that ... It is expected that ...'. Banish them. They can only stop you developing your potential as a writer.

Make sure that you really are getting personal. It is usually not enough to include people by referring to categories. When a firm sends us a letter referring to 'Our valued customers', it leaves us cold. We certainly don't feel valued. When a council sends out a note with the words 'Ratepayers are reminded ...', we don't feel involved. As for 'The library is open to the general public between 9 a.m. and 8 p.m.', it sounds as if even the riffraff will be allowed in at certain hours. We wonder what it has to do with us.

Incidentally, how would you react to 'We offer you, our valued customer, a chance to win a free trip to Paradise Island'? It certainly makes it clear that it's a form letter. A more personal alternative would be 'We value the business you've given us over the years so we're offering you a chance to win a free trip to Paradise Island'.

Name drop. Be a gossip. Wouldn't it be more interesting to say that Jane wrote the report, that it was Peter's holiday in France that left us shorthanded this month, that Jim and Kylie repaired the pipe in the middle of the night and that it was Mrs Elsie James in Frenchs Forest who wrote the letter saying they were a couple of real heroes?

Which of these alternatives is personal? Which do you prefer?

A	B
1 It will be appreciated that four persons would not be enough for a staff party.	Clearly, four of us would not be enough for a staff party.
2 Our engineer has checked it and believes that the site would be dangerous in a strong earthquake.	Investigations have shown that the site would be dangerous in a strong earthquake.
3 It is believed that the new wedding management service will begin advertising by the end of the month.	We believe that Sara Jones will begin advertising her new wedding management service by the end of the month.
4 You sent us more than we need to license your three dogs.	The envelope contained more money than necessary to license three dogs.
5 The project is programmed to begin in two months. Further information can be obtained from this company's head office.	We will begin the project in two months. If you need more information please contact Janet at our head office.

The personal sentences are 1B, 2A, 3B, 4A, 5B. Easy, wasn't it?

■ PUTTING THE FIVE KEYS TO WORK

Let's put the five keys to effective writing to work in a range of everyday business letters.

Over the next few pages, you'll see examples of letters on typical topics. Don't be distracted by the subject matter. The examples show different ways of thinking about business writing. Concentrate on the differences in style.

The best test is to read each aloud. (Go on. They'll get used to it! So will you.) Ask yourself: which is more precise, makes you want to read on or (where it's appropriate) builds relationships and gives better service?

REPLY TO A CUSTOMER'S COMPLAINT

Without using SIDAP (Simple, Informal, Direct, Active, Personal)

 Dear Mr Jones
SLOW DELIVERY

With reference to your letter of March 2, we thank you for drawing our attention to the matter of the delivery time.

We give an assurance that the circumstances are being investigated with a view to instituting improvements to our service in future. We also wish to state that such a delay in delivery is contrary to our policy.

In recompense, we offer a gift voucher equivalent to the value of the articles mentioned. We wish to apologise for any inconvenience.

Yours faithfully

MPSmith

M. P. Smith
CUSTOMER SERVICES MANAGER

How would you feel about the reply and the company that sent it?

Notice the formality and the detached, impersonal style. Mr Smith misses an opportunity to win back Mr Jones's support. He uses formal language and doesn't even mention the product that arrived late. It's indirect and gives Mr Jones the impression that this is just another formula letter.

Let's take a different approach.

Using SIDAP

Dear Mr Jones

SLOW DELIVERY

Informal, personal	Thanks for taking the trouble to write to me about the slow delivery.
Simple, direct	I agree. It should not take five days to deliver a pair of gate hinges.
Personal, direct	I apologise for the inconvenience it caused you. It was well below our usual standard and we are finding ways to ensure it doesn't happen again.
Personal, active	I hope you will accept the gift voucher as some compensation, and that you will use it soon so that you can experience our (usually) excellent service.
Personal, informal	Please contact me personally if you ever have any concerns about our delivery in future.
Informal	Sincerely

Informal (he's used his
first name, not initials)

Michael Smith

Michael Smith
CUSTOMER SERVICES MANAGER

LETTER TO A POTENTIAL CLIENT

This first draft is cold and stilted. It's a string of formal clichés.

Not using SIDAP

X Dear Mr Jones

OFFICE CATERING

With reference to your response dated March 3 to our advertisement in *The Tabloid* on February 25, please find enclosed a copy of our brochure for your perusal.

This company has been in business since 1980 and has a proud tradition of service and this has been complimented by businesses of all sizes in this city during this time.

We appreciate your interest in our services and take this opportunity to assure you of our best attention at all times, should you wish to proceed.

Thank you for your reply.

Yours faithfully

PMSmith

P. M. Smith
SALES MANAGER
BUBBLES CATERING LIMITED

Using SIDAP

 Dear Mr Jones

OFFICE CATERING

Simple, informal, direct, personal

Thank you for replying to our advertisement in *The Tabloid* and your interest in our catering your end-of-year party.

Informal, personal, direct (specific)	Pages 15 to 20 of the brochure have suggestions for office parties and some of the ways we could help. You'll find the price list on pages 21 and 22.
Personal, direct	Think of us as the people who can take the worry and stress out of organising an office party.
Personal, simple	I would be delighted to talk through your plans with you.
Informal	Sincerely
	Peter Smith
Informal	Peter Smith MANAGING DIRECTOR BUBBLES CATERING

REPLY TO AN UNSOLICITED LETTER FROM A JOB SEEKER

Not using SIDAP

Dear Mr Jones

EMPLOYMENT ENQUIRY

We acknowledge receipt of your letter with enclosures and your request for an appointment to discuss employment.

We are, however, not in a position to offer you a vacancy at the present time.

Vacancies do arise on occasion and we wish to keep your documents on file. If you have any objection to this course of action please contact the undersigned.

Sincerely

TM Smith

T. M. Smith
MANAGING DIRECTOR
GLOBAL TRADE LIMITED

Would you still want to work for them? You could think this firm is led by a cold fish, but it's just as likely that he's a warm-hearted softy who just needs to use the five keys to effective writing.

Using SIDAP

✔

Dear Peter

EMPLOYMENT ENQUIRY

Simple, informal, direct (specific) — Thank you for your letter asking about vacancies in our sales team.

Informal, personal, active — At the moment we have all the sales staff we need, but I was interested in your experience and will certainly let you know when we are ready to advertise another vacancy.

Simple, active — I would like to keep the copy of your CV in the meantime, but please call me if you want me to return it.

Informal — Sincerely

Terry Smith
MANAGING DIRECTOR
GLOBAL TRADE LIMITED

LETTER TO THE BUILDING OWNER

Not using SIDAP

✘

Dear Sir

LEVEL 4 TOWER BUILDING

Further to our telephone conversation of July 24, we advise that we have now perused the lease document to determine which party is responsible for repairs to the electrical water heating system.

Pursuant to clause 8 in the First Schedule and clause 10.1 (a), it would appear that the responsibility does in fact lie with the occupiers of the building.

We therefore accept responsibility and will pay the account submitted by Ajax Plumbing Limited in due course and wish to extend our appreciation for your courtesy in this matter.

Yours faithfully

J. M. Smith

J. M. Smith
OFFICE MANAGER

Using SIDAP

Dear Sir

LEVEL 4 TOWER BUILDING HIGH STREET

Informal, simple

Thanks for the discussion about who pays for the repairs to the water heater.

Personal, active, direct

I have checked through the lease and your recollection was correct. It does put the responsibility on us.

Simple, active

We will pay the bill from Ajax Plumbing.

Informal, personal

Thanks for handling our misunderstanding so amicably.

Informal

Sincerely

Janet Smith

Janet Smith
OFFICE MANAGER

LETTER OF EXASPERATION

Not using SIDAP

Dear Sir

INVOICE: 4715

This company rejects claims in your recent letter with regard to the above invoice and urges further consideration by your company of recent correspondence on this matter.

Perusal of those documents will reveal that we are not in debit to your company and that, on the contrary, our account has been in zero balance since the goods in question were supplied and returned as unsuitable, a credit note having been obtained. We have since sought other suppliers with a standard of service more commensurate with our needs.

Thus, we see no value in entering into further correspondence with you and indeed urge you to take what legal remedies you might believe are open to you. It must be stated, however, that any legal action over this matter will be defended with vigour and our solicitors will ensure that an application for appropriate costs is applied for.

Yours faithfully

J. M. Smith

J. M. Smith
MANAGING DIRECTOR
LIGHTNING SERVICES

Perhaps this writer believes that pompous language will make his letter sound tough. But the talking-to-the-nation formality does little more than make him seem aloof, even hostile. Being specific and coming right out with it (being direct) would have helped him present his argument more effectively.

Using SIDAP

	Dear Mr Jones
	INVOICE: 4715
Simple, active	We have received your letter advising that unless we pay your account for $1240.31 you will take legal action.
Simple, informal, direct, active, personal	It is the last straw. We returned your insulators months ago and have a credit note to cover the invoice.
Personal	I must give you a summary of this frustrating affair. It may help to improve your relations with customers in future.
Active, direct, personal	**March 3** You sent us the insulators and an invoice. We called your Service Manager, Miss Williams, to say that they were damaged and we were sending them back.
Active, direct, personal	**March 11** As arranged, Miss Williams sent a credit note for the full amount and a letter of apology.
Active, direct, personal	**May 16** We received an account for overdue payment and rang your office. I spoke to Mr Lee, who said he would cancel the overdue notice.
Simple, active, direct, personal	**June 14** Another account arrived. I rang both Mr Lee and Miss Williams explaining that we had returned the insulators. Both

	apologised and said they would take action immediately. I faxed a copy of the credit note to Miss Williams.
Simple, active, direct, personal	**July 20** You sent a reminder. We ignored it.
Simple, active, direct	**August 5** You sent your 'final reminder'.
Direct (comes right out with it)	It seems that your system failed because no one followed through.
Direct (comes right out with it)	This company pays its bills. We have been tolerant and courteous, but that time is up. We will only answer any further demands for payment in court and will certainly apply for costs.
Direct (comes right out with it)	We believe that you owe us an apology.
Informal	Yours sincerely
	John M. Smith
	John M. Smith MANAGING DIRECTOR LIGHTNING SERVICES

■ AN EASY WAY TO EDIT YOUR WRITING

The five keys to effective writing give you an easy way to edit your work. Most untrained writers have no focus to their editing. They don't have anything specific to look for, so they just keep changing the words around until somehow the writing seems better. You can be much more effective than that. Ask yourself constantly, 'Could it be simpler, more (appropriately) informal, more direct, active or personal?'

PRESCRIBE CURES

We can make the process even more efficient.

Below is a poorly written draft from a previous example that I'm editing using the five keys. The letters represent the keys, so each is a prescription, not a criticism. *A* means 'It could be more active', *P* means 'It could be more personal'.

Notice, too, that I haven't corrected the draft. You don't need to either because you already know how to make writing simpler, more informal, direct, active and personal. Don't slow the process down by making changes on paper — just do that as you retype.

Sometimes you can think of more than one prescription in the same line. In this example, the first two lines could be more personal, direct and informal, so I have used the symbols P, D and I.

PDI
AI — This company rejects claims in your recent correspondence with regard to the above invoice and urges further consideration by your company of recent correspondence on this matter.

I — Perusal of those documents will reveal that we are not in debit to your company and that, on the contrary, our account has been in zero balance since the goods in question were supplied and returned
DA — as unsuitable, a credit note having been obtained.

ID — We have since sought other suppliers with a standard of service more commensurate with our needs.

I
P — Thus, we see no value in entering into further correspondence with you and indeed urge you to take what legal remedies you might believe are open to you. It must be stated, however, that any legal action over this matter will be defended with vigour and our solicitors
A — will ensure that an application for appropriate costs is applied for.

Don't worry if you didn't spot all the flaws in the draft or if you have a slightly different interpretation. It doesn't matter. Ironically, the imprecise nature of this editing system is what makes it so efficient. Because the keys overlap, making a sentence more personal will usually make it active and more informal as well. Making a sentence simpler will often also make it more direct.

Effective writing is a frame of mind. Just prescribing one key in a paragraph will probably be enough to get you back into writing in a style much closer to a business conversation with the reader. You might find that you are not just changing words, but whole paragraphs and that the words are flowing naturally.

■ IMPORTANT POINTS WE'VE COVERED IN THIS CHAPTER

- You are already skilled in a complex, subtle language. All you have to do now is use that skill in specific ways.
- The golden rule of all communication is: be audience-centred.
- The real differences between average and effective writing are *the five keys to effective writing: Simple, Informal, Direct, Active, Personal.*
- Effective writing is about communicating — it's not about blindly following writing conventions.

Chapter 2

Holding their attention

- Building rapport

- Give them variety

- Make it flow

- Give it rhythm

- The Rule of Three

- Contrast

- Not only ...

- Don't go away

- The power of the last bit

'The same week our fowls were stolen, Daphne Moran had her throat cut.'

Got your attention? That's how Ronald Hugh Morrieson begins his novel *Scarecrow*. Would you read the next paragraph?

Of course, we can't go making up stories about people having their throats cut just to attract the attention of our readers. But we can copy the technique. Morrieson's opening line is short, direct and engaging. Ours should be too. Most business letters don't grab attention; they encourage us to scan the whole letter in search of something to persuade us they're worth the effort.

> *We are arranging a seminar at our premises on July 26 at 5.30 p.m. for the purpose of explaining what the changes to the tax depreciation policy announced by the Government recently will mean for our major customers.*

Eyes glazing over? How about this instead?

> *Good news.*
> *You might have less tax to pay next year. The Government's announcement on depreciation will help most companies like yours, some considerably, some only slightly.*
> *Would you like to hear more?*

You can go on to give the details of where and when. The key difference is in the way we attract the reader's attention. In the first draft we cram it all in. In the second, we begin with a short statement and feed the readers more information when they are ready for it. Notice that we use *you* and *yours* to make it more audience-centred and personal.

Most writers begin with formal clichés.

> *Further to our telephone conversation of March 12, we advise that ...*
> *In reply to your letter of May 17, my specific interest is in ...*
> *I refer to our correspondence at the end of August and ...*

Break out. Talk to them on paper. And here's a bonus: it's much easier to write openings that grab your reader's attention.

> *Thank you for your letter on Friday. I agree. We will have to do something about the maintenance.*
> *Thanks for the meeting on Tuesday and for your interest in hearing more about our hygiene service.*
> *Thanks for letting me know how well the study program is working out for you.*

It was good to hear from you on Wednesday. I was especially interested in your comments about John's success this year.

Thank you for your proposal. We accept.

Thanks for the demonstration last week. It's certainly an impressive machine and we would like to know more.

I thought you might appreciate a written record of our discussion on Tuesday.

Your fax came as a complete surprise.

If you are initiating the contact, get straight to the point, but keep it conversational.

What I am about to say might surprise you.

I'd like to talk frankly with you.

I'll make this brief, but it's important. Did you know that five of our branch managers are away this week with stress-related illnesses?

I have been thinking about your comments on Thursday. You were right, and we must take action immediately.

We are going to help you make more money this year — even if you don't do business with us.

I have some disappointing news for you.

We hope you can join us for a celebration.

Let's hold their attention too.

Ever been stuck with the party bore? Ever wondered what makes them so boring and you so conscious of the time, your backache and your struggle to maintain focus?

The party bore is generally self-absorbed. An interesting guest is interested in other people too, including us, and quickly develops rapport. The party bore is usually obsessed with facts. The interesting conversationalist is genuinely interested in feelings, impressions and opinions; yours as much as theirs. The party bore drones. The interesting guest offers us a variety of pace and topic. They keep coming up with surprises. We can be interesting in our business letters, reports and presentations too.

■ BUILDING RAPPORT

Nothing builds rapport as effectively as the golden rule of all communication — be audience-centred. Never lose sight of the reader's interests, needs and motivation.

Don't tell your readers or audience what they already know. It wouldn't be audience-centred. Here's an important rapport-building principle:

Acknowledging shared understanding builds rapport.

Let's take an example. You could use that cliché, 'Please find enclosed our brochure'. But the reader knows the brochure is there. It's bigger than your letter and probably fell out of the envelope on to the desk. 'Please find enclosed ...' says you don't know that your reader has already found it. A rapport-building alternative would be, 'You'll find the high performance model on page six of the brochure'. You are saying in effect, 'I know you have found the brochure and I remember that you were particularly interested in the high performance model'. You are acknowledging a shared understanding.

By the same reasoning, you can build rapport by leaving out some details. Usually you don't need to say, 'Thank you for your letter of March 17, outlining the problems you have had with our service department between February 14 and 28'. You could say, 'Thank you for your letter. I have spoken with the service team and ...' In effect you are saying, 'We both remember what the letter was about'.

Yes, but what if they don't remember what the letter was about? The context will tell them. Or, if there's likely to be any doubt, add Ref.: Letter March 17 on the right, above your text. It looks bureaucratic but it allows you to separate the paper trail issues from the body of your letter so that you are free to talk to your reader about things they don't know.

Many people worry that if they don't say 'Please find enclosed' and they forget to put the brochure in, the reader won't know to ring them and ask for it. If you refer to your brochure in the letter your reader will know, but you can always put it beyond doubt by adding '*Encl.: brochure "Better Building Products"*', after your signature.

Always avoid telling your readers or audience what they already know. Instead, refer to it and move on.

■ GIVE THEM VARIETY

Vary the length of your sentences and paragraphs. It can make an enormous difference to the visual appeal of your letter and your reader's motivation to keep reading. Give them variety in your presentations too. Varying the length of sentences and paragraphs will make them sound more appealing.

President John F. Kennedy knew the value of varying the length of sentences. Here's what he told rapturous Berliners at the height of the Cold War.

'There are many people in the world who really don't understand, or say they don't, what is the great issue between the free world and the communist world.
   Let them come to Berlin!
   ... And there are even a few who say that it's true that communism is an evil

system, but it permits us to make economic progress.
    Lass' sie nach Berlin kommen! Let them come to Berlin!'

It's regarded as one of the finest speeches of the 20th century. The variety in the length of sentences helps to make it easy to absorb and it even looks inviting in written form.

So what does Kennedy's speech have to do with business writing? Let's apply the idea of a long sentence followed by a short one to a business context.

You asked me to keep you up to date with developments, so I want to mention that next Friday our managing director will be speaking to clients with a particular interest in packaging for Asian markets.
    Would you like to come?

You can do the same with paragraphs.

Joan has shown the real value of having an operations manager with the skills and maturity to bring out the best in people, under pressure. In her five years with us she has always been focused on the goals of the company, yet has been a patient listener and even a confidante for many of the people in her team.
    We strongly recommend her.

Long, short is a pleasing effect, but don't let it become predictable. How about long, long, short occasionally? Variety is the key.

Always be looking for surprises. What can you tell your readers or audience that changes their view of your theme? What interesting and relevant new ideas can you add?

■ MAKE IT FLOW

I like to picture my readers floating downstream in a canoe. I want to give them the most effortless journey possible, so I aim to remove all the rocks from my writing. Here's a real estate sentence with rocks.

Constructed with brick and plaster finish, it is a well maintained, mature, established home built 35 years ago, and enhanced and refurbished with every modern comfort.

Let's remove the rocks.

It was built 35 years ago in brick and plaster and its current owners have refurbished it with every modern comfort.

It flows because the ideas in the sentence are connected.

Here's one that could have come from a company newsletter:

Bill, who has been our Chief Executive since joining us from Acme Biologicals Ltd (where he was engaged in marketing some ghastly parasites) in 1997, says he has never seen the company in better shape.

Notice how it uses commas and brackets to introduce ideas that interrupt the sentence. No reader should have to work so hard. Let's eliminate the irrelevant ideas and connect the essential ones in a way that flows:

Bill has been our Chief Executive since 1997 and says he has never seen the company in better shape.

Remove anything that interrupts or diverts your reader or audience. Be especially careful if you are writing a presentation, because if it doesn't flow the way conversation does, you will draw attention to the fact that you are simply reading a prepared text. Remember Winston Churchill. The British Parliament allows MPs to use notes but not to read their speeches, and members will shout 'Reading! Reading!' if they do. Yet Churchill read all his speeches and even close colleagues who had been involved in some part of the preparation found it hard to believe that he was not speaking off the cuff. Yes, he was a fine performer, but he also knew how to make the written word flow naturally.

There's no better test of flow than reading aloud.

UNNATURAL FLOW	NATURAL FLOW
Built in 1877, the immigration building was used by Captain Robert Scott to prepare for his final journey to the Antarctic.	The immigration building was built in 1877. Captain Robert Scott used it 30 years later as he prepared for his final journey to the Antarctic.
Having formerly operated from Wordsworth Street for 25 years, we are now moving.	We have been at Wordsworth Street for 25 years, but we are now moving.
Managed by us since 1984, the fund has since become one of this country's most popular fixed-term investments.	The fund has become one of this country's most popular fixed-term investments since we took over its management in 1984.

The examples on the left put the reader on hold before getting to the point. Many such sentences are clumsy, especially when you read them aloud. For some reason, people who write tourist and real estate brochures love them.

■ GIVE IT RHYTHM

Rhythm?

Yes. The best writing has rhythm. Rhythm works most dramatically in presentations but will help you in even the most ordinary letter. It will certainly help you hold their attention. Probably the most common rhythmic pattern is the list.

'With this faith, we will be able to work together, to pray together, to struggle together, to go to jail together, to stand up for freedom together, knowing that we will be free one day.'— Martin Luther King

'Let every nation know, whether it wishes us well or ill, that we shall pay any price, bear any burden, meet any hardship, support any friend, oppose any foe, to assure the survival and success of liberty.' — President John F. Kennedy

They are the historic words of orators, but you can use the same technique in letters and presentations and no one need know that Martin Luther King or President Kennedy inspired you.

Imagine this in a presentation to a departing staff member:

'Thank you for your dedication to the project, the confidence you have given us, and the enthusiasm you leave behind you. We value them all.'

Or in a letter to a slow payer:

We have sent you three written reminders, telephoned you four times, asked our solicitor to write to you and heard all your assurances. You have still not paid the account.

■ THE RULE OF THREE

Lists of three usually work even better. It's the *Rule of Three*. The human mind finds something especially satisfying about lists of three. That's why we have 'Goldilocks and the Three Bears' and 'The Three Little Pigs', and why many jokes depend on three events.

Let's find some business examples.

We need to meet, agree on a plan and contact every one of our customers. John has set an example to us all with his outstanding energy, determination and leadership.

> *You'll be able to use this software for all your reports, graphics and spreadsheets.*
>
> *Let's get this deal negotiated, signed and under way before the end of March.*

You can use the Rule of Three simply for a satisfying rhythm. You can also use it to take control and rivet attention to your message. It depends on the context and the ideas you choose to list. Try the Rule of Three at a meeting some time.

You can add an enhancement, a *pay-off*. It's a comment about the list of three. You'll need an example to see what I mean.

> *We need to meet, agree on a plan and contact every one of our customers.*
>
> The future of the company depends on our success.

Here's a striking example of how the Rule of Three and a pay-off can be made memorable. The New Zealand television camera operator Margaret Moth was shot in the face while working for an American network in Sarajevo. She was interviewed for television as she recovered from an operation on her jaw. She made this comparison with American friends who expected to be wealthy in their retirement:

> *'I've been down the Amazon in a canoe. I've crossed the Sahara on a camel. I've been shot in Sarajevo. Those are my riches.'*

Don't think of it as a technique just for orators. Margaret Moth's injuries prevented her raising more than a whisper so they put her words on the screen in case we missed them. Use the Rule of Three in your presentations, letters and even conversations. It's a powerful way to communicate.

■ CONTRAST

There's something particularly appealing about contrasts.

> *'I come to bury Caesar, not to praise him.'* — Mark Antony in *Julius Caesar*

> *'We observe today not a victory of party, but a celebration of freedom.'*
> — President John F. Kennedy's opening to his inauguration speech

> *'See what a scourge is laid upon your hate, that heaven finds means to kill your joys with love.'* — The Prince addressing the crowd over the bodies of Romeo and Juliet

Politicians love contrasts. It's understandable because, for some reason, audiences in political rallies feel obliged to applaud when they hear them. If people clapped every time you used a contrast you'd keep using them, wouldn't you? Why not use the same technique in your letters, reports and memos? Your readers probably won't break into applause, but they will read on.

Let's have some business examples:

I want to remind you that the taxi chits are for staff who work after 8 p.m., not for those who simply miss their ride home.
The response was not the five hundred letters we had expected, but five thousand.
I found the report was very critical, yet surprisingly perceptive.
We are still negotiating my fee. It's not the numbers we are arguing about, it's where to put the decimal point.

■ 'NOT ONLY ...'

Here's a very effective way not only to accentuate the contrast, but to build a rapport with your audience.

Hillary Rodham Clinton used the *not only* technique at the Democratic Party convention of 1996. As the delegates prepared to endorse her husband as their candidate for president of the United States, she told them:

'... it takes a president who believes, not only in the potential of his own child, but of all children. It takes a president who not only holds those beliefs, but acts on them.'

Notice how she accentuated the contrast with the words *not only*. Did they applaud? Of course.

Now here's the subtle bit. Let's imagine that you are a lawyer writing to a client and you use the *not only* technique this way:

I have looked through the records your aunt left with us and found, not only her will and the financial statements, but also a letter, and it's for you.

You have highlighted the surprise of the aunt's letter, but you have also done some subtle rapport building. You are also saying, 'I know that you knew the will and financial statements would be there'. Remember that acknowledging shared understanding builds rapport.

Useful? Certainly.

Imagine now that you are the head of your organisation writing to all your staff. You could use the *not only* technique to build rapport.

We will be replacing our computer system in March. It's not only unreliable; it's costing far too much to maintain.

You are telling them that you know that they know it's unreliable, but you go on to tell them something that they didn't know — that it's costing too much to maintain. You are acknowledging shared understanding and following it with a surprise.

Of course, it's possible that some people on the staff didn't know that the computer system was unreliable. They do now, and you've also told them in a way that helps your relationship with those who did know.

So now you have a device to help you inform those who don't know, build rapport with those who do, come up with a surprise, enhance the contrast and achieve a satisfying rhythm. Not bad for two words.

■ DON'T GO AWAY!

There's another way to hold their attention, though I have to warn you that in written form it only comes in industrial strength. It's the enticer, a one-sentence paragraph that says, 'Don't go away, there's something really interesting coming up!'.

Enticers work well in sales letters and in most presentations. Imagine that your readers are just about to lose their concentration and you come up with one of these lines:

Here's the surprising part ...
Here's the most important point ...
Let me explain that ...
It's surprising, but it's true and here's why ...
But there's one point I want to stress ...

EXAMPLE: enticers (they are in italics)

Good Morning Mr Sparrow.

What I am about to say might surprise you. A recent survey of thousands of businesses, worldwide, has revealed that most businesses can double their profits without having to spend any more on advertising. It's just a matter of encouraging more existing customers to come back.

> *Here's the really surprising part.*
>
> The survey showed that all it takes to double profits is five per cent more repeat business.
>
> It seems amazing. Like me, you are probably sceptical about surveys. Would it help if I point out that this survey was conducted by Bain and Company and the Harvard Business School? The finding is clearly very credible and the implications for all of us in business are enormous.
>
> *Let me explain that.*
>
> For most businesses ...

It's hard to stop reading letters like that.

■ THE POWER OF THE LAST BIT

Every sentence and every paragraph should end strongly. The last bit is no place for insipid writing. A weak ending will show much more than a weak middle. A strong ending will hold your readers' attention and reinforce your message.

Let's compare to make the point.

WEAK ENDING	STRONG ENDING
At 13, Vanessa Mae recorded the Mendelssohn and Tchaikovsky violin concertos and became the youngest person in the world to record these. We are surprised that you have neither replied to our letter nor paid the account. Please contact us immediately so that an arrangement for payment can be devised. I am pleased to let you know that the company has decided to donate $2000 in response to your application for assistance.	Vanessa Mae was the youngest person in the world to record the Mendelssohn and Tchaikovsky violin concertos. She was just 13. We are surprised that you have neither replied to our letter nor paid the account. Please contact us immediately. Thank you for your application. I am pleased to let you know that the company has decided to donate $2000.

On the left, we have endings with vague words, passive statements and unnecessary words. On the right, the endings emphasise the main point. They are either short or they contain a powerful image or important information.

Another example of using the power of the *last bit*:

'More Americans die every year from smoking related diseases, than from AIDS, car accidents, murders, suicides and fires ... combined.' — President Bill Clinton announcing measures against the marketing of cigarettes to children (August 1996)

■ IMPORTANT POINTS WE'VE COVERED IN THIS CHAPTER

- Make the opening line short, direct and engaging.
- Involve your reader from the first line.
- Build rapport by acknowledging shared understanding and referring to or leaving out what your reader knows.
- Vary the length of sentences and paragraphs.
- Make it flow by removing anything that interrupts or diverts your reader or audience's attention.
- Give it rhythm with lists, the Rule of Three and a pay-off.
- Use the power of contrast.
- Use the *not only* technique to build rapport, add surprise, enhance contrast and achieve a satisfying rhythm.
- Use enticers to lead readers or audiences into your next point.
- Give your sentences and paragraphs strong endings.

C h a p t e r 3

Persuasive ways

- Pre-empt objections

- How open should you be

- Painting pictures

- Persuade with the power of analogy

- Using the golden rule

- Ask for action

- Making it memorable

I often ask people in my workshops to describe typical salespeople. Out come the clichés: 'untrustworthy, insincere, greasy, pushy, looking after number one'.

'But we are all in sales', I tell them. There's usually only a slight pause then a smile or two. They know what I'm getting at. The accountants, the engineers, scientists and secretaries might not have thought about it as selling, but they all sell ideas. Teachers sell ideas, lawyers do, so do mums and dads with teenagers. Even the teenagers sell ideas, such as why it's really far safer, and more socially acceptable, to have a car than a bike.

Is it useful to agree that we are all in sales?

Yes. If we are in the same business, let's find out what professional salespeople do and adapt their methods to our letters, reports, proposals, presentations and even conversations. While we are at it, let's do the same with the techniques orators and marketing people use.

I'm not suggesting that you should adopt a slick, hype-laden, insincere style that reads or sounds like a sales script or imitation oratory. But pick up the techniques and then apply them in language that's right for you and your readers or audience.

First, let's note something about modern professional salespeople, the ones who sell the higher value products and services for a living. Selling and salespeople are changing fast, especially in business-to-business selling.

Even in car sales you are less likely to meet a hyena in a loud jacket and mirror sunglasses slapping you on the shoulder as he says, 'Have I got a great deal for you!' Career salespeople are far more interested in discovering our needs and matching them than in twisting our arms. They have to be more sophisticated, because as buyers we are. They also know that they can earn enormous rewards by selling to us in a way that earns our trust and builds a long-term relationship. As writers, we are just as interested in being audience-centred and building relationships.

■ PRE-EMPT OBJECTIONS

It used to be a 'well known fact' in selling that the more objections prospective customers raised, the more likely they were to buy. The research shows it's not true. A far more effective way of selling an idea is to pre-empt objections — in other words, to answer them in advance.

So how can you use the principle of objection pre-emption?

First, be clear about your proposal. Then imagine you are your readers. Why wouldn't they accept your argument? What objections might they raise? What objections might they be thinking of but not tell you? What have they said before on the subject?

Let's take an easy one. Let's imagine that you want to persuade your management team to start every working week with an organised social hour for all the staff, first thing

Monday morning. You can imagine the objections. Give some thought to how you might pre-empt those objections.

POSSIBLE OBJECTIONS	PRE-EMPTING THE OBJECTION
It would be a waste of work time.	We'll be enjoying ourselves, but we'll still be working. We can use the time to think together as a team, focusing on our goals for the coming week.
	We would be spending the best part of the first hour socialising around the photocopier anyway. This way we'll make that time more productive.
They'll come to work drunk.	We won't provide alcohol.
It won't achieve anything.	People are more productive if they can form networks outside their own departments.
There'll be no one to answer the phones.	We will roster two different people to sit in for the receptionists each week.

Notice that in the process we've modified the proposal. Often when we examine possible objections we realise our proposal isn't saleable in its present form. We can be sure, for instance, that a social hour with alcohol on Monday morning wouldn't fly and it's better to abandon that part of the proposal before it destroys the rest.

■ HOW OPEN SHOULD YOU BE?

You usually have to make a choice with objections: will you bring the objection out into the open or not?

For instance, you might be writing a proposal for a prospective client who knows very little about your company, your company's reputation and the quality of its products and services. The objection forming in the prospect's mind is, 'I don't know these people so I don't know whether to trust them'.

To state the objection you might write, 'You might be wondering whether we can be trusted'. Clearly, that's not a good idea. Sometimes your judgement tells you that putting the objection into words might create a negative memory. Instead, just show that it doesn't apply. You might want to tell your prospective client how long your company has been in business, list some of the more important projects your company has completed and quote some comments from delighted clients. It's not always important that the objection be stated, only that it be pre-empted.

✔

Dear Peter

REPLACING THE VEHICLE FLEET

I have been thinking about your comments on the standard of our vehicles and your concerns about the cost of replacing them.

At the next management meeting, I'm going to recommend that we sell all our executive and sales cars and lease replacements.

Pre-empting an objection

Leasing will remove the problem of raising capital to buy new cars. In fact, we could probably release $1.6 million by selling the existing fleet.

Pre-empting an objection

You might be wondering whether leasing would cost us more. It wouldn't, if we take into account that we can use the money more efficiently for the new power system, or the marketing campaign in Europe. We wouldn't need to borrow for either project and we would have some tax advantages from leasing the cars.

Pre-empting an objection

In case you are wondering whether it's the right time to change, I should pass on Anna's comments about the fleet. She says the maintenance bills have increased 30 per cent in the last year and she's convinced that the smaller cars are not suited to the distances the sales staff are doing now.

Give me a call if you would like to talk it through in more detail.

Regards

Jocelyn Smith

Jocelyn Smith
OPERATIONS MANAGER

■ PAINTING PICTURES

Martin Luther King was in sales. So were John F. Kennedy and Winston Churchill. They knew how to sell an idea. The formal language of their oratory won't help us write better letters, reports and presentations, but their selling skills will.

Picture this. It is August 1963. The civil rights leader Martin Luther King looks out from the steps of the Lincoln Memorial in Washington DC. Before him are two hundred and fifty thousand Americans. The television cameras and cluster of microphones reveal that the world is watching and listening. Martin Luther King's emotions surge as the crowd responds to the first few minutes of his carefully prepared speech. He abandons his notes, finds new inspiration and as his voice soars out over that crowd, he creates history with pictures.

> *'I have a dream that one day down in Alabama, with its vicious racists, with its Governor having his lips dripping with the words of interposition and nullification ... one day right there in Alabama little black boys and black girls will be able to join hands with little white boys and white girls as sisters and brothers. I have a dream today.'*

The crowd's reaction is stunned silence, then tumultuous applause. Notice the pictures, particularly the picture of the children. In the same speech he spoke of his dream that '... one day on the red hills of Georgia, the sons of former slaves and the sons of former slave owners will be able to sit down together at the table of brotherhood'. Painting pictures is a standard technique of oratory.

So how can we use pictures in business writing and presentations to staff or clients?

It's easy. Provide details that build mental pictures but keep the images simple. Paint pictures your readers or audience can relate to. Avoid contrivances. Use all the keys to effective writing. Being specific is *direct*. Get *personal* by telling your readers or audience who was there and what each person did and said. Make your language appropriately *informal* and your pictures won't come across as imitation oratory. They will persuade.

EXAMPLE: painting pictures

Dear Mr Smith

SOFTWARE INSTALLATION

I need to put on record our dissatisfaction with the software your company has installed for us. It has not lived up to the promises in your proposal and the whole experience has been frustrating and costly.

Your technical team has been testing and correcting for five weeks but the system remains unreliable and continues to disrupt our business.

Let me give you an example.

This morning I arrived at my office to find two of your technical staff had taken over the system for testing. By 8.30 our office staff were at their desks and expecting to use the system. It was still 'off line' but your technicians assured us that they would have it back in action within a few minutes.

By 9.00 we had sales staff calling from branches all around the country wanting to know what was happening. Altogether they had already handwritten hundreds of packing slips and receipts for customers, which they would have to type into the system later.

By 9.15 your team was still at work and still promising to have the system ready within a few minutes.

At 9.25 we had to stop production at our factory in Lane Cove. Fifty-three staff sat in the staff room while our suppliers continued to arrive with truckloads of raw materials we could not process.

The system was back on line by 10.05.

We have had to put up with breakdowns every three days on average.

I must now ask you to ring to make an appointment so that we can discuss urgent action to upgrade the system, or remove it.

Sincerely

Claude Jones

Claude Jones
MANAGING DIRECTOR
FRESH FOODS CORPORATION

■ PERSUADE WITH THE POWER OF ANALOGY

Martin Luther King's picture of the children holding hands is not only a word picture but an analogy, because it encourages us to make a connection with a wider argument about racism. Analogy is another favourite device of orators, but it's no modern invention. It wasn't even original when Jesus gave us the parable of the Good Samaritan.

Choose your analogy well and you'll have a powerful tool of persuasion. Often a graphic and relevant analogy will be far more persuasive and memorable than a detailed argument.

President Franklin Roosevelt used an analogy when he wanted to persuade Americans to help Britain with the lend-lease program in 1940.

'Who of you, if you saw your neighbour's house was on fire, would not lend him your hose to put out the fire?'

Yes, we would certainly lend the hose, and suddenly helping a nation by lending ships seems more acceptable.

In the House of Commons, Winston Churchill denounced appeasers of Germany with the line, 'An appeaser is one who feeds the crocodile, hoping it will eat him last'. A graphic picture and a persuasive analogy.

In 1946 Churchill added a handwritten line to his speech to Westminster College in Fulton, Missouri.

'From Stettin in the Baltic to Trieste in the Adriatic, an iron curtain has descended across the continent.'

It wasn't original. He had even used it before himself, but it suited the occasion. There's much more substance to the speech than that memorable image, yet it's often referred to as, 'Churchill's Iron Curtain speech'. It became a cliché and journalists and politicians were still using it four decades later.

But beware. An analogy is only justified if it fairly represents the wider argument. If you are comparing a rival firm to an ageing elephant make sure that it is big and old and knows nothing about modern ideas of service or management.

EXAMPLE: pictures and analogies

MEMO TO STAFF

I keep being reminded of just how much it costs to run our branch.

Specific examples paint a picture.

Last month we were almost $200 over our budget on telephone calls, $250 over on stationery and more than $300 over on general expenses, including postage, courier firms and even cups of tea and biscuits.

Analogy.

At times, it's like trying to run the wrong way on a conveyor belt while someone turns up the speed.

I would really appreciate your help in keeping our overheads down.

Paula Smith

Paula Smith
MANAGER

Notice the analogy comparing the rising costs of running the office to running the wrong way on a conveyer belt. All the examples are specific, and relevant to the readers.

■ USING THE GOLDEN RULE

Let's pick up some ideas from the direct marketers. Okay, so they're the people who send us those letters we don't want, about products or services we don't need, but don't dismiss them. The best direct marketers are skilful persuaders.

Successful direct marketing is a science. The marketers use a range of techniques and measure the success of each variation. You can adapt their ideas without your writing seeming insincere or pushy.

The direct marketers know their golden rule of all communication — *be audience-centred*. They often refer to it as 'What's in it for me?' and the successful ones never lose sight of it. They sell benefits (what their product will do for us), not features (the characteristics of their product). So they should. Usually, we don't ask to be on their mailing lists. If we're going to give their letters more than a glance, they have to show us from the beginning that there's plenty in it for us.

They use special phrases to highlight the ways we'll benefit.

This amazing window washer can reach up three storeys and bends so that you can clean even the skylights without a ladder.

Notice how the phrase 'so that you' highlights the benefit for the reader. It also provides a discipline for the writer to stay audience-centred.

This respected magazine comes to you each week so that you can have regular briefings from people who specialise in keeping close to the market.

Persuasion has to be audience-centred. Anything else is irrelevant.

We will be replacing the XT81 with the ZP25, so that you can have enough memory for the modern graphics software.
We will close the production line on Tuesday afternoon so that you can come to the end-of-year barbecue.

You can emphasise 'What's in it for me?' even more strongly by combining a 'you' phrase with a question.

You might be wondering what's this got to do with me?
You'll be asking yourself what's the connection between the changes in the exchange rate and our future in exporting?

A 'you' phrase and a direct statement can work just as well.

You might be wondering *how the changes will affect you. The first change
    you'll notice is ...'*
You're probably thinking *I wouldn't do anything dishonest ...'*

Successful direct marketers talk to us on paper. The most skilful achieve a conversational style that makes us think they are people like us, people we can relate to. Using words like *you, yours, I, we* and *ours* helps you to achieve that style. Write it just as you would say it, but with polish.

■ ASK FOR ACTION

If you want them to take action you have to come right out with it. Tell them what you want done. Never just provide the facts and hope your readers or audience will reach the conclusion you want and then get around to doing something about it. Make it easy for them to say yes and take action immediately.

It can be difficult to decide when to ask for action. If you are making a major selling push to a resistant audience, it would be best to leave it until you have pre-empted all the objections. But then you must ask them to act.

■ MAKING IT MEMORABLE

Ideally, you want to persuade them for life. You certainly want them to remember your argument long enough to act on it or persuade other people with it. Let's use a little psychology on memory and learning. You'll find it particularly helpful for presentations, especially to large groups.

Studies show that visual imagery works well. Most people have a better memory for pictures than words alone, so painting pictures helps make your key points memorable. It certainly worked for Martin Luther King and Winston Churchill.

Psychologists have also found that emotion and memory are linked. Many believe that some moderate emotional arousal is an essential ingredient in learning or remembering. Showing *what's in it for us* helps to raise our emotional level, but you can add emotion to most pictures without seeming artificial, simply by talking about humans and their feelings.

A memo to staff expressing displeasure:

*Frankly, Michelle and I were embarrassed to discover just how badly we'd let the
Highland Corporation down with our delivery, yet as a company we had been so
confident in our promises and so proud of our record. It's time to act, and act quickly.*

An opening to a presentation to people who help others find jobs:

'I was unemployed myself once.

It was in 1972 and it was only for a week. You'd say that I was just between jobs, but I had a young family, a large mortgage, and years of specialised training I was desperate to use. It was a frightening experience.

Today, when I see young people get a job, often after months of worry and struggle, it evokes in me an emotional response that I'm sure stems from that one week.

I want them to succeed, so I want you to succeed, and I'm delighted to be here this morning to make a contribution.'

A letter to a management team:

You can imagine Peter's feelings when he came to work the next morning. He'd worked 16-hour days on the New Flavours project, personally saved it from disaster several times and shown extraordinary determination and creativity over four months. Then, when it succeeded so spectacularly, nobody expressed a word of appreciation.

We can give much better leadership than that. We can, and must, give credit where it's due. Always.

I often ask people to tell me their strongest recollection of television images of the Vietnam war. Almost all of them have seen the news coverage, if only in documentaries. One image comes up every time. It's not footage of combat, or even B52s; it's the little girl running away from her village, her back burned by napalm. She is screaming with pain. Emotion makes ideas and images memorable. It also makes them persuasive.

Don't be shy with emotions. Just use an appropriate level of feelings or emotion, so that you are comfortable with it and your readers or audience accept it as accurate in the context. Anything more is propaganda, but emotions belong as naturally in written English as they do in conversation.

Keep in mind that most of us can only retain about seven chunks of information in our short-term memory at any one time. (The size of the chunk depends on, among other things, the motivation of the reader.) When we reach our limit we start replacing what we've already heard with new chunks. Be economical with your arguments. It's not what you tell them that counts. It's what they remember.

■ IMPORTANT POINTS WE'VE COVERED IN THIS CHAPTER

- We are all in sales, so let's learn from the professionals.
- Pre-empting objections is a powerful tool of persuasion.
- Paint pictures to persuade.
- Use the power of analogy.
- Use the direct marketer's focus on 'What's in it for me?'
- Talk to your readers on paper.
- Use appropriate feelings to make your arguments persuasive and memorable.
- Most people can only retain about seven chunks of information in their short-term memory, so be economical with your arguments.

Chapter 4

Writing proposals and reports

- Proposals — all in the preparation

- Organising reports and presentations

Reports and proposals are both persuasive documents. Proposals are obviously so, but even in reports you'll most likely be showing why your readers should accept your recommendations or your perspective on events. Everything we've covered so far is relevant to reports and proposals, but we need to look at some additional techniques that could significantly improve your success rate.

■ PROPOSALS — ALL IN THE PREPARATION

Writing effective proposals is easy. The real work is in the preparation.

So how do you prepare? Here's a quick course in relationship selling. It's a client-centred approach to selling and draws on the findings of the Huthwaite Research Group, which studied 10,000 salespeople in 23 countries and discovered what the most successful sellers do.

Let's imagine that you are representing a printing company. Most printing companies base their proposals on price but you are looking to offer value, and price might not be the most important element of the customer's notion of what gives them best value. Asking the right questions could make a very big difference to the way you write your proposal.

First, get the client to reveal their needs by asking about their problems or opportunities — and not just the obvious ones. (It's the same process, whatever the product, service or idea you are selling.)

YOU	YOUR PROSPECTIVE CLIENT
How well is your current printing service working out?	Well, we use a couple of printing companies. They're alright but we've had a few problems.
Can you tell me more about those problems?	One missed a deadline a few weeks back, the other doesn't keep in touch so we never really know if they are going to deliver on time.
What other problems have you had?	The quality was good but they were expensive — both of them.

Now get an idea of how important the problems (or opportunities) are to your client.

YOU	YOUR CLIENT
You mentioned that one missed a deadline. What effect did that have?	Well, it was a major problem that time. They were leaflets for a mail-out we were planning and it had to coincide with other things. If they had been even one day later we would have had to scrap the whole thing. Deadlines are usually a big issue here.

You also mentioned that the current suppliers are expensive. Compared with quality and delivery, how important is price to you?	Important, but not as important as the standard of the job and the timing. We probably wouldn't go to a cut price merchant and risk quality and delivery, put it that way.

Now suggest a possible solution and test its value to the client.

YOU	YOUR CLIENT
If we were to guarantee our quality, give you progress reports and deliver on the agreed date or reduce our fee by 20 per cent, to what extent would that overcome the concerns you've had with your current suppliers?	That would do it. I'd want the guarantees in writing and we would have to agree on which ones are major jobs, but your price would have to be right too.

So far you have picked up that your client needs certainty. That's a big part of their perception of value. It's more important to them than price. You could exceed (slightly) the price of their current suppliers and you would probably still get the job.

WHAT DISADVANTAGES WOULD THERE BE?

Disadvantages?

Yes, there's no better way to pick up objections. If you think that's a bit negative, let me tell you about a company in earthmoving equipment. The company's salespeople wanted to sell a bulldozer and quarrying equipment to a new client. Even before they had made a proposal the client seemed keen to buy and could tell them several benefits. Then one of the sales team asked, 'What disadvantages would there be if we were to offer the equipment we've talked about?' It's not traditional selling, but the information it produced was extraordinarily valuable.

'Well, there would be a problem,' said the quarry owner.

'What's that?'

'I've got a shed full of parts out the back. They're all for other makes. They've cost me a fortune and if I buy your equipment they're not going to be any use to me.'

'Anything else?'

'Yes. I've got a new worker here. He's a young man with a family. If I go ahead with this I'll have to send him down the road. I don't want to do that.'

'Okay', said the sales team, 'we'll see what we can come up with.'

In their written proposal they were able to tell the quarry owner that they would buy the parts for the other brands. They could sell them on to larger clients who operated a variety of machines. The objection had disappeared.

They couldn't save the young employee's job, but they could soften the impact.

They would link him up with a firm that specialises in helping people who have lost their jobs. That objection was eroded.

Asking for the disadvantages can save sales — if you know what to do with the answers.

You need to get in early and ask about possible disadvantages before you write your proposal, letter or presentation.

WHAT TO INCLUDE

Now the easy part of your proposal. First, you have to make a decision. Is it simple enough for a letter format or will you need a full proposal in a bound booklet with a covering letter? Both formats should have some common features that will make full use of the valuable information you picked up in your discussion with the client.

- Report your understanding of the client's needs.
- Summarise what you are offering.
- Report the benefits and any disadvantages your client saw in your solution.
- Show how you will achieve the results the client needs and overcome any disadvantages of your solution.
- Tell your client what it will cost and your terms of payment.
- Express an interest in the project, working with the client or solving the problem.

Reporting is an important concept. You can use phrases such as 'When we spoke on Wednesday you mentioned that ...' It makes it clear whose idea it was. You are helping the client continue the process of selling to themselves, and they are the ones who have to be convinced.

If it is a full proposal, report the needs with headlines such as 'Our understanding of your needs'. If you are using the letter format, you could say 'Let's begin by ensuring that we have a clear understanding of your needs. I remember you making the following key points ...' Too informal? Try it, and watch your clients smile as you take them through the list. Informally reporting your understanding of their needs builds rapport.

Here's a hint. Be slightly conservative about their needs. Your clients know that it's in your interests to play up their needs, so being a little conservative is a quick way to build trust.

An extract from a formal proposal:

✔ **OUR UNDERSTANDING OF YOUR NEEDS**

From our discussion with Jason Smith and Tanya Jones on June 10 we understand that you have four major needs:

- to have print deadlines met without exception

- regular progress reports on major print jobs
- quality at least to the standard of your current suppliers
- a reasonable price.

In a full proposal you should provide a summary on the first page. Summarise your solution, the problems the solution would overcome and the benefits the client told you about.

Apply the nosey parker test of a good summary.

Think of someone who knows nothing about your proposal seeing it lying open on your client's desk and try to make it so crisp, relevant and interesting to the passer-by that they will want to pick it up. Make it so short that they will be able to read it before your client returns. Even if it never happens that way, it's a good discipline to adopt.

You should also add relevant supporting information about your company's record, perhaps with references from previous clients, summaries of similar projects, perhaps some profiles of your key people. Tell them about your company's special qualities: its reputation for service, its understanding of the local market or its experience as a problem solver.

Always tell your clients you will be in touch, and call to see if the proposal was what they were expecting. Keep calling until you get a decision.

Here's the beginning of a proposal in letter format:

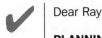

Dear Ray

PLANNING THE COMPANY'S FUTURE

Thanks for the discussion last Wednesday and the opportunity to propose training and facilitation for your staff.

Let's begin by ensuring that we have a clear understanding of your needs. I remember the following key points.

- You need to involve all your staff in planning your company's development.
- You need to have them own the eventual plan and ensure that they play an active part in putting it into action.
- You need to produce a Corporate Directions document by June 30 next year. It would be an outcome of the workshops we are proposing. The Corporate Directions document would become the primary focus of all your annual business plans.

■ ORGANISING REPORTS AND PRESENTATIONS

Here's an easy and logical way to assemble your facts, evidence and arguments, so that both you and your reader always know how everything fits together.

Let's use an analogy. Try thinking of the contents of your report or presentation as a city your reader doesn't know.

1. *You'll want to provide an introduction by describing what kind of city it is, especially the reason for its existence. With a report or presentation that means you'll be stating its purpose.*
2. *Next, think of the suburbs within the city. They give more detail about the nature of the city and why it exists. The suburbs of your report or presentation are the main topics.*
3. *Then, think of the streets. They are the details contained in each of the suburbs.*

Imagine that you only have a few disjointed ideas about what to put into a report and no idea how to organise them. The city analogy will help you brainstorm and organise your thoughts into a logical structure. You should be able to do most of it in ten minutes. See Chapter 5 for a template for this method.

Sceptical? Try it. All you'll need are, say, 30 slips of paper, about one centimetre by three (or small *Post-its*) and a coloured pen.

Start at street level. On each slip write a note about any idea that might be useful in your report. A word or two should be enough to remind you later.

Go as fast as you can, with just one idea per slip. Don't censor, just keep the brainstorming going. Think of facts, arguments, objections you could pre-empt, quotes, evidence and even anecdotes that might be relevant.

When you have run dry, start organising the streets into suburbs. Which ideas go together? Arrange them in columns. Are there any gaps you could fill now or with some research? Note them on the remaining slips and slide them into place.

USING THE CITY ANALOGY TO ORGANISE YOUR REPORT OR PRESENTATION

Give each column a heading and use the coloured pen to separate it from the streets.

Give your report a city view with a brief statement about its purpose.

Now here's the real beauty of the system. Once you have the slips in place, you can move them around. You might decide, for instance, that an idea would be easier to explain if you dealt with it under another heading, so you just move it into the suburb you want. You might want to change the order of the suburbs. It's easy.

The city analogy allows you to keep track of how the various elements of your report or presentation relate to each other. You start with brainstorming — simply writing anything that might be relevant or useful on separate slips. Then you move the slips around until you have the most logical structure. You'll probably find that creating suburbs and thinking about the streets makes you think of other streets or suburbs you could add.

Here's one way to structure a standard report. Think of them as 'suburbs'.

- Introduction
- Summary
- The methods you used
- The results of your investigation
- Your conclusions or recommendations

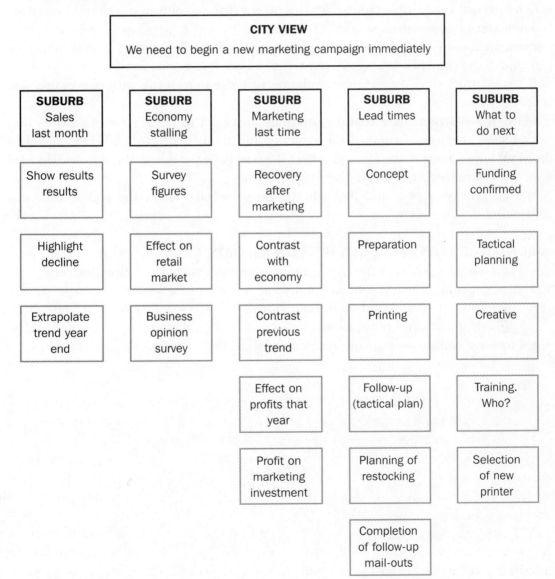

CITY VIEW
We need to begin a new marketing campaign immediately

SUBURB Sales last month	SUBURB Economy stalling	SUBURB Marketing last time	SUBURB Lead times	SUBURB What to do next
Show results results	Survey figures	Recovery after marketing	Concept	Funding confirmed
Highlight decline	Effect on retail market	Contrast with economy	Preparation	Tactical planning
Extrapolate trend year end	Business opinion survey	Contrast previous trend	Printing	Creative
		Effect on profits that year	Follow-up (tactical plan)	Training. Who?
		Profit on marketing investment	Planning of restocking	Selection of new printer
		Completion of follow-up mail-outs		

Write a covering letter reminding the reader of the reason the report was requested, the topic and acknowledging the contribution of other people.

PROVIDE A CONTEXT

Imagine that you are suing a business competitor for using your trade name. He's taking a valuable slice of your business away — so valuable that if you can't stop him immediately the bank will send in the receivers. You are asking the court for damages to help you recoup your substantial losses. The judge writes 50 pages of carefully reasoned legal argument and her decision is, as judges' decisions always are, at the end. Your fate is in her report. Could you read the legal argument first and absorb it, or would you need to know the outcome first?

Even when there's less at stake, we need to know where the report is leading before we can absorb the contents. We just have to. It's the way our brains work.

If it's your job to make a recommendation or a decision, break with convention and supply it first.

Many report writers have told me that they are asked to put their recommendations last to show that they examined the evidence and thought it through before making a decision. Surely most readers would expect them to have thought it through and decided on their recommendation before they began writing.

You can always repeat and highlight the recommendation at the end as a formal statement.

IMPORTANT POINTS WE'VE COVERED ON REPORTS

- For a longer report, use the city analogy to ensure that it has a clear, logical structure and to help you brainstorm what you need to cover.
- You could give your report an introduction and summary, then describe your methods, results and conclusions.
- Provide a context — put your recommendation first.

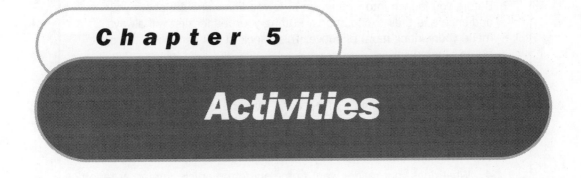

Chapter 5

Activities

- Checklists

- Templates

- Activities

If we want our readers to sit up and take notice we have to be serious about the golden rule of all communication: being audience-centred. Before you launch into writing, be sure you know enough about your audience and their expectations. Putting your reader first will always make your writing more effective. This checklist will get you in the right frame of mind.

1. How well do you know your reader? Are you on first name terms?

2. Should you be?

3. Does your reader speak formally on the phone or in person?

4. What does your reader want from your letter, article, memo or report?

5. How interested is your reader?

6. What does your reader need — specific information, assurance, support or encouragement?

7. How does your reader feel about you and your organisation?

8. Does your reader know less than you about the subject — and accept the difference in knowledge?

9. Is your reader more interested in facts and figures than relationships or emotions?

10. Does your reader have a preference for summaries or details?

11. Does your reader share your sense of humour?

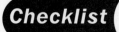

Here's a useful summary of the five keys. You might like to refer to it as you try Activities 1 to 5 (on SIDAP).

Simple

- Fewer words.
- Simpler words and ideas – even if you need more words.
- Simpler constructions.

Informal

- Appropriate informality.

Direct

- Come right out with it!
- Be specific.

Active

- Active = Actor + Verb (in that order).

Personal

- Write about people and things, not just things.
- Use you, I, we, your, our.

Feel free to copy this template for use in organising your reports or presentations. Remember the city analogy: start off with a city view; narrow it down to a number of suburbs; and then fill the suburbs with street detail.

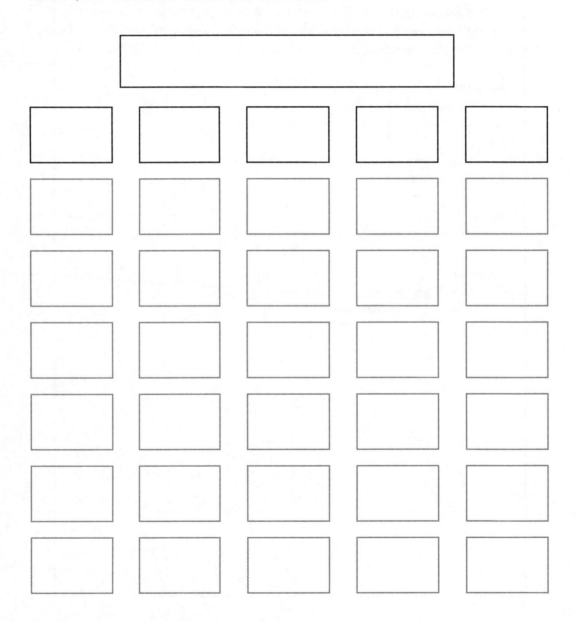

Templates are time-savers for those routine letters or emails, but most are stuffy. Make them appropriately informal. It's not always necessary to make them personal in the sense of appearing to be written especially for the reader, but it's better service and easy to do.

Ensure that you review them regularly. It's surprising how easily they can get out of date in subtle ways, and you can sometimes be horrified to discover that they've been sent out for months with wording that now makes you wince.

Dear ....

Thank you for your application for ....

We received it on .... and we expect to have a decision for you by ....

If you have any additional information or any questions about the licensing process please call the committee secretary .... on .... It's a direct line.

Sincerely

Dear ....

Thanks for your .... I have completed the forms for you but need your signature on pages .... before we can go ahead.

I suggest that you read the contract carefully before you add your signature.
Please keep the yellow copy in a safe place and send the white and green copies back to me as soon as possible.

Our head office staff usually take less than two working days to process the applications and I will call you to let you know when the funds are available.

Sincerely

Activity **1** *Simple*

Simple is the first of our five keys to effective writing. Using fewer words and simpler constructions usually improves written communication. Try applying this principle to improve the sentences below.

1. After having endeavoured for some eighteen months to effect some broad-spectrum improvement in our worrisome affairs, the directors are pleased to announce a discernable upturn in our performance.

_____

_____

_____

_____

2. Although Mr Marks has always been and is still a highly valued member and esteemed representative of our club, there is no denying that he has knowingly failed to attend three consecutive games and, in terms of our rules, must therefore be subject to censure.

_____

_____

_____

_____

3. John Orr's would like to take this opportunity to announce to the public at large that its spring line will be modelled at an exclusive fashion parade at its city store in High Street on 3 June.

_____

_____

_____

_____

See page 76 for some suggestions.

Many of us were taught to write in formal, stock phrases that we have learnt as Commercial English. In fact, this inhibits communication more than it helps it. Practise speaking to people on paper by providing informal equivalents for the following.

1. After initial small group discussions participants were encouraged to select a spokesperson to report their findings to the entire assembled group.

_____

_____

_____

_____

_____

2. Mr and Mrs Barnaby Henders of 'Glen Innes' at 5 Kilgarren Place hereby cordially extend an invitation to Mr and Mrs K. H. Bell and family of Enderby to the celebration of the wedding of their elder daughter, Kerry-Anne, to Matthew, younger son of Mr and Mrs P. J. Cottgold of Shropford.

_____

_____

_____

_____

_____

See page 76 for some suggestions.

Direct is our third key to effective writing. It means being specific and saying what we mean. Of course, it's possible to be *too* direct. Sometimes you'll want to soften your writing to be more diplomatic, but that's very different from hiding your meaning and asking the reader to discover it.

Try to make the following extracts as direct and specific as possible.

1. I have some concerns about the company's projected revenue stream in the next few months and flag the possibility that it may have a detrimental effect on our plans for expansion.

_____

_____

_____

_____

_____

2. The City Council has received numerous reports of failure to conserve water —
particularly in outlying suburbs; even those associated with increased fire hazard.
The Council staff have noted that water reservoirs are lower than optimal for this time of the year.

_____

_____

_____

_____

_____

See page 76 for some suggestions.

Activity 4 — Active

Remember the simple formula for active sentences: Active = Actor + Verb (in that order).

Following the formula will have a dramatic effect on your writing. How would you breathe life into the following by rewriting them in their active form? While you're about it, try replacing the verbs with more vigorous ones.

1. Consideration has been given to your proposal for a canteen on office premises.

   _____

   _____

2. An inquiry was conducted into the methods employed by those running the drug trials.

   _____

   _____

3. Use should be made of the blank sheet at the end of the application for information about criminal charges.

   _____

   _____

4. It would be appreciated if you would forward your replies to the coordinator without delay.

   _____

   _____

5. The cancellation of the play program would devastate the many needy children who depend on it for recreation.

   _____

   _____

See page 76 for some suggestions.

Activity 5 Personal

Getting personal means writing about people. It means using words such as *you, I* and *we* and the names of relevant people. Show how the objects, events, regulations, even scientific concepts are relevant to humans. Personal is the big one because getting personal usually makes your writing active and almost always more informal and direct. If however you are not sure what's wrong with your first draft, try personal.

Try adding more people to the following sentences — especially your readers.

1. The defaulter will be liable for every day in which this failure continues to a fine of $200 or to 20 hours of community service.

   _____

   _____

2. It is with regret that we inform our customers of the discontinuation of this line of merchandise. Stanton Foods hopes to be able to publish a list of replacement products for diabetics by the end of the week.

   _____

   _____

3. Employees applying for this in-house transfer will be informed of the dates of their interviews within seven days.

   _____

   _____

4. Prospective foster parents would not only be helping children at risk, they would certainly also be enriching their own lives and those of their family members enormously.

   _____

   _____

See page 76 for some suggestions.

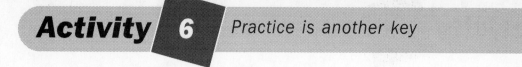

It's one thing to see the SIDAP keys applied in these pages and another to start using them yourself. How can you best apply the five keys to effective writing to your own written communication? This activity is a good place to start.

What to do

1. Look for some letters, proposals or reports you have produced recently. Choose writing with different audiences and different purposes. Are there some you know didn't have the desired effect on their readers? Be sure to include them.
2. Review them using your editing skills. Write S, I, D, A or P in the margins to note how they could be improved. It will make the rewriting more focused and save you time. Think of each letter as prescribing a cure.
3. Rewrite some sentences following your editing instructions, SIDAP.
4. Now compare. Can you see a big improvement — achieved relatively easily?

What to look for

Stay focused on the golden rule (be audience-centred) and the five keys (SIDAP). They will cure most lapses in effective writing. If you extend the list, you are likely to be describing the same problems in a range of different ways and you will lose focus quickly.

Does your organisation have an in-house style or templates? A standard response, particularly with letters you and your colleagues write regularly, saves time and ensures that people are treated equally. Unfortunately, most standard responses are stored on computers and are rarely reviewed. Many are written in *commercialese*.

What can you do?

What to come up with

1. Think of how you might persuade others in your organisation of the benefits of writing more effectively or altering templates or report formats.
2. Use SIDAP and the golden rule of all communication to create some alternatives to show your colleagues.
3. Which templates/formats/house rules are most in need of revision?

What to consider

1. Are there any members of your team you could enlist to help you change your organisation's written communication?
2. Can you think of some test cases you could take on to prove that writing effectively works?
3. Is there a media liaison or human resources department that would be a good place to start selling the benefits of the five keys to effective writing?

Try this

Set an example. Change your own style of written communication to reflect your new skills.

Activity 1: Simple

1. Our directors report that their efforts are paying off. They have announced a discernible improvement in our performance.
2. We must censure Mr Marks. He is still a valued member but has broken the club rules by missing three consecutive games.
3. John Orr's invite you to see their exclusive spring fashion parade at the High Street store on June 3.

Activity 2: Informal

1. We asked each group to appoint a spokesperson to tell us what they discussed.
2. We hope you can join us to celebrate the wedding of our elder daughter Kerry-Anne and Matthew Cottgold. (End with your names and address.)

Activity 3: Direct

1. I'm worried that if we don't improve our sales soon, we will not have enough money to pay for our expansion into Europe.
2. The City Council's engineers report that the water levels in the reservoirs are lower than they should be at the beginning of the fire season. They say that people are still wasting water, even in the suburbs at greatest risk from bush fires.

Activity 4: Active

1. We have considered your proposal for a canteen on office premises.
2. The professor conducted an enquiry into the methods the scientists were using in their drug trials.
3. You should use the blank sheet at the end of the application to provide us with information about criminal charges.
4. The committee would appreciate your forwarding your replies to the co-ordinator without delay.
5. If we cancel the program the many needy children who depend on it will be devastated.

Activity 5: Personal

1. You will be liable to a fine of $200 or 20 hours of community service for each day you fail to pay.
2. We are sorry to tell you that we have had to discontinue this line of merchandise. We hope to provide you with a full list of replacement products by the end of next week.
3. If you have applied for this in-house transfer, we will call you within seven days about a date for your interview.
4. You will find that fostering children-at-risk also enriches your life. Your whole family will benefit from the experience.

Chapter 6

Sample letters

- Bills — theirs and yours

- Customers and suppliers

- Employment issues

- Colleagues and friends in business

- Miscellaneous

- Last word

◼ BILLS — THEIRS AND YOURS

Courtesy and directness will get you everywhere.

Late payers might be frustrating, but you'll get your money faster if you resist temptation. Consider the power balance alone. They have your money and if they refuse to pay, you will have the inconvenience and expense of taking them to court to get it. Cold, impersonal letters, demands or an aggressive tone just encourage many people to hold out a little longer.

Probably more important, they might pay, but go elsewhere next time. Is it worth the short-term pleasure of expressing your frustration over, say, a couple of hundred dollars when in the next five years the same customer might pay you a couple of thousand dollars in repeat business?

Examples begin on the next page.

PLEASE PAY IT NOW

Make the first letter light and assume that the failure to pay is simply an administrative hiccup. You should always give the details the accounts staff will need to track the account down. Address your letter to a person, not just a department. Make your letter personal too, and go back to the same person each time.

Dear Mr Jones

OVERDUE ACCOUNT

I need your help.

Somewhere in your department one of our accounts has been waiting for payment for more than a month. Could you rescue it?

Aardvark and Company is one of our most valued customers and you have always paid our accounts promptly in the past. I would appreciate your paying this one as soon as possible.

The invoice date is February 27. The number is 574671 and the amount $2945.63.

Thank you.

Sincerely

Larry Smith

Larry Smith
MANAGING DIRECTOR
THE BREAD COMPANY LIMITED

PAY UP — PLEASE!

Maintain your combination of courtesy and directness. The words 'I plan to call you at the end of this week' will encourage your reader to take a personal interest.

Dear Mr Jones

OVERDUE ACCOUNT

We need some urgent action on an overdue payment.

Do you remember that I wrote to you on May 1 about our account for $2945.63? It is now almost two months overdue and we have not seen a cheque or heard from you.

The invoice date is February 27. The number is 574671.

I plan to call you at the end of this week but I would appreciate a cheque before then.

Thank you.

Sincerely

Larry Smith

Larry Smith
MANAGING DIRECTOR
THE BREAD COMPANY LIMITED

FINAL REMINDER

This time go straight to the top.

Dear Mrs James

OVERDUE ACCOUNT

We have struck a serious problem in our business relationship and I need to ask you to take a personal interest.

We have sent your accounts department two reminders to pay an account dated February 27.

They were addressed for the attention of Paul Jones.

Mr Jones did not reply and his assurances on the telephone came to nothing.

Unless we receive your cheque by July 5 we will close your account and ask our solicitor to take action.

The invoice number is 574671.

Naturally, we would be delighted to see our business relationship back to normal before then.

Please pay the account or call me if you need to discuss it.

Sincerely

Larry Smith

Larry Smith
MANAGING DIRECTOR
THE BREAD COMPANY LIMITED

WE HAVE ALREADY PAID YOU

Dear Mr Smith

INVOICE 86263

Thank you for your letter about invoice 86263.

I have checked our records and bank statements and it is clear that we have paid it.

The cheque number was 0753125, issued on May 6 and marked 'not transferable'. Our bank statement shows that it was cleared from our account on May 10.

Please call me if you need any more information about it.

Sincerely

John Adams

John Adams
SENIOR ACCOUNTS OFFICER
ABACUS CORPORATION

YOUR INVOICE IS INCORRECT

You might be irritated by the error, but good relationships with suppliers are valuable. It's worth being at least civil. It's especially important to make your letter direct, so be specific about administrative details, and clear about what is wrong and what you want done. If you don't already know it, it's worth asking your supplier's receptionist for the name of the person who handles your invoices.

Dear Mrs Jones

INCORRECT INVOICE

I need your help with two errors on invoice AV674210.

You'll see from the quotation that Jones Print quoted $847.00 for printing our letterheads but on the invoice the figure is increased to $957.00.

The invoice also lists artwork, but we supplied the artwork. The quote was simply for the printing.

We would appreciate a credit note for $957.00 to cover this invoice and a new invoice for $847.00.

Sincerely

Jasmine Smith

Jasmine Smith
OFFICE MANAGER
ABACUS CORPORATION

Encl.: quotation for letterheads, copy of invoice.

■ CUSTOMERS AND SUPPLIERS

You can set your organisation apart by being human. Leave the stuffy language for the contracts and your competitors. Use appropriate informality and personalise your letters so that every letter reflects the beginning or a renewal of a relationship.

You will want to keep it simple, direct and active as well, but you should aim to have your readers say, 'These people are good to deal with'. It's good business and good service.

WE ACCEPT YOUR QUOTE

Lighten up. You might be announcing the result of an important decision but you have everything to gain by showing that you are a good person to deal with.

Dear Mr Jones

CONSTRUCTION OF STORAGE SHED

We accept your quotation for the construction of our storage shed.

Your price of $81,256.00 plus GST was not the lowest, but we were impressed by your company's experience and references. We also appreciated your quick response to our invitation to put in a proposal and we're looking forward to seeing the storage shed built with similar efficiency.

We need to attend to the paperwork as soon as possible. Please call me to make an appointment next week.

Sincerely

William Smith

William Smith
MANAGING DIRECTOR
H. L. SMITH AND SON LIMITED

WE'RE MOVING

Many businesses, when they change address, simply announce the new one, missing an opportunity to develop the relationship with their customers.

This is also a time when your business is vulnerable. When you change location your customers might wonder whether your new location will be convenient for them or if it's even worth the trouble of changing their records.

Be audience-centred and overcome any objections in advance. It's an excellent time to review your service so that you can offer them something new in your letter as an incentive to contact you soon. You could even offer a discount on their next purchase, or a chance to win a prize.

Dear Mr Jones

BIG NEW STORE AT ST IVES

We are about to make it even more rewarding to be a Prestons client.

You'll discover some important changes when you come to our new store at St Ives. We're confident that we'll be offering you the best range of protective clothing in the city and the most comfortable, convenient way to select clothing.

Here's our new address from April 13:
    15 Barker Avenue
    St Ives
    SYDNEY

You'll see from the map that our new store is just 100 metres south of the overbridge and there's plenty of customer parking.

Our telephone and fax numbers are the same. I hope you'll call in soon and make use of the discount voucher.

Yours sincerely

Leonard P. Smith

Leonard P. Smith
CUSTOMER SERVICES MANAGER
PRESTONS CLOTHING LIMITED

WE CAN'T AGREE WITH YOUR COMPLAINT

Complaints are the biggest bargain in marketing. People who complain are doing you a service. Most unhappy customers just go elsewhere and might tell everyone they know why they'll never come back. People who complain *to you* give you a chance to put things right.

Stating the facts isn't enough. People who complain are expressing their feelings. It's very important to acknowledge the feelings as well as the facts.

If you ignore the feelings you will leave your customer unhappy. Your letter should show that you have taken a personal interest in the complaint. See your reply as a chance to rebuild a damaged relationship even if you feel you have done nothing wrong. It's the customer's perception that counts.

Dear Mrs Jones

Thank you for your letter telling us that you were unhappy with the prices of the air flow meters and connector hoses.

I was concerned that you found the prices much higher than you expected and showed your letter to our general manager of customer services, Jayne Mitchell. We checked the prices and found they were correct. We also checked the prices several of our competitors are charging. Not only were our prices slightly lower, but we were the only company in our modest survey to include an extended guarantee.

I do understand your frustrations with rising costs, but I believe that our combination of high quality products and service gives excellent value overall.

Thank you for being a valued customer for more than five years, and for giving us the opportunity to reply.

Sincerely

Joseph Smith

Joseph Smith
SENIOR CLERK
ENGINEERING SOLUTIONS LIMITED

YES, YOUR COMPLAINT IS JUSTIFIED

Acknowledge the feelings as well as the facts, and imagine you are talking to the customer in the same room.

Most people send out formal letters with very little that's specific to the complaint. Such letters suggest that they didn't read the complaint and perhaps that their organisation gets too many of them to treat complaints separately.

Show a personal interest. Make it simple, appropriately informal, direct and active. Be open in your apologies and generous in making amends. Most people who take the trouble to complain can be persuaded to remain a customer. They just want their complaint taken seriously and their feelings acknowledged.

Dear Mr Smith

Thank you for your detailed letter about the frustrations you have had with the 6.45 p.m. bus from Courtney Square.

I certainly agree that we failed you. The bus left five minutes before the advertised time on all three days. I can only assure you that it was a genuine mistake by a driver who was helping out while your regular driver was on sick leave. We are changing our system to ensure that we brief our relief drivers more thoroughly.

We are disappointed that we let down one of our most loyal customers, but we appreciated hearing from you so that we could correct the problem. We cannot take away the inconvenience, but I hope you will use the concession cards so that we can restore your confidence in our service.

Sincerely

Ronald Jones

Ronald Jones
OPERATIONS MANAGER
SWIFT TRANSPORT LIMITED

Encl.: five concession cards.

IT'S NOT GOOD ENOUGH!

Righteous indignation can be satisfying, but if you want results from your complaint, be direct. Give enough detail to help with the supplier's investigation so they have no excuse if they send you back a bland reply. Even a complaint can be in conversational language. Aim for appropriate informality.

Dear Connie

HELP DESK SERVICE

We have had some problems with your 'help desk' service this month. I need to discuss them with you in the next few days and thought you would want to see the details first.

We have been logging our calls to the help desk since the problems began.

- On April 16, 18, 25 and 29, several of our staff were kept on hold for up to five minutes.
- On April 16 and 29 two of our staff reported that operators spoke to them rudely, seemed reluctant to take their calls and would not give their names.
- On April 18 I called and asked for your help desk supervisor. She was out and did not reply to my message to call back.

Your staff do seem to be under pressure, but we can't continue to use your service if it does not improve.

I will be in touch.

Sincerely

Ray Jones

Ray Jones
PROCESSING MANAGER
FINANCIAL INVESTMENTS LIMITED

Dear Fiona

GELATINE

Thank you for sending us the brochure. We found it a useful introduction, but we have some specific questions.

- Is your gelatine suitable for the machines we plan to use to produce our confectionery range next year? (The leaflet gives the machine's specifications and performance.)
- Can Gelatine World guarantee at least 150kg of gelatine per week from February 1 to December 14?
- Is the current price guaranteed for at least a year?

I will contact you in the next week so that we can talk over each of the questions I have raised.

Sincerely

Jocelyn Jones

Jocelyn Jones
PROPRIETOR
ADVANCE CONFECTIONERY

Encl.: specifications for XA305 confectionery machine.

WOULD YOU LIKE TO VISIT?

Dear Jocelyn

GELATINE PRODUCTS

I have been thinking about our conversation on Friday.

Would you find it useful to visit our factory? You would be able to see how we make the gelatine and assure yourself of the quality. I can also show you our latest technology.

I have spoken to our engineering manager, Anna Packard, and she would be very pleased to meet you and discuss any concerns you might have about quality or delivery.

If you'd like to come, just give me a call on ext. 7663. I'd be happy to arrange it.

Sincerely

Fiona Smith

Fiona Smith
SALES REPRESENTATIVE
GELATINE WORLD

THANKS FOR THE EXCELLENT SERVICE

Make your praise as specific as your complaints. Being specific is direct, the third of our five keys to effective writing. And name names — that's getting *personal*.

Dear Mr Jones

I am one of those customers who are very willing to complain about poor service, so it's only fair that I should also acknowledge excellence.

We rang last Friday to arrange for a large parcel to be delivered across town. It was four o'clock and our client needed it before five.

Susan Kingston took the call and understood the urgency immediately. She arranged for Tony Travis to pick up the parcel within a few minutes, then Peter Turner rang us back at about five to five to assure us that it had arrived.

We rarely ask for special treatment but when we needed it your team seemed delighted to take over our problem. They are a credit to you.

Many thanks.

Sincerely

Clyde Smith

Clyde Smith
OPERATIONS MANAGER
INDUSTRIAL INSTRUMENTS LIMITED

YOUR ACCOUNT IS NOT JUSTIFIED

Give enough background for your letter to stand alone — so that your supplier does not need to find the previous correspondence to understand it. Be direct, keep it simple, and be clear about what you want.

Dear Mrs Smith

DISPUTED INVOICE

Thank you for your reply to my enquiry about a 23-minute call to Japan on April 3.

I was surprised to see that you have decided not to change your account.

We did not make the call and believe that we should not have to pay for some failing in your system.

We have paid our accounts promptly for the five years we have been in business. We have never contested any amount. You might ask yourself why we would suddenly choose to protest about an account for $30.88.

We know the account was incorrectly addressed. The credibility of your billing system is at stake and your company should contact the person who took the call in Japan to verify our claim.

We believe that you should credit $30.88 to our account and assure us that you have fully investigated the lapse in your system.

Yours sincerely

Percy Jones

Percy Jones
ADMINISTRATION MANAGER
GENERAL METALS LIMITED

WE ARE NOT PAYING THIS!

Dear Mr Jones

INVOICE 56352

I am returning a copy of your account for repairs to our fax machine. We will not be paying it.

You might want to review your service when you read our reasons.

Our office manager called your firm around 10 a.m. on May 14 to say that our fax would not take incoming calls. She asked for an urgent response because most of our clients' orders come by fax.

Your serviceman arrived at 4.30 p.m., made no apology for being late and took a quarter of an hour to examine the machine before saying that your company does not repair our brand.

The travelling time is equally unjustified. Your receptionist should have told us that you do not repair our brand and we could have called another firm immediately. You would not have incurred the cost of travel and we would not have had to put up with the delay.

We believe that you owe us an apology and a credit note for the full $75.86.

Yours sincerely

Peter S. Smith

Peter S. Smith Ph.D
CHIEF EXECUTIVE
CAMDEN BIOLOGICALS LIMITED

SORRY WE GOOFED!

Be open about the mistake. Apologise and acknowledge the customer's feelings.

Dear Dr Smith

INVOICE 56352

We do indeed owe you an apology and a credit note.

We take pride in our service but it is clear that in your case it was well below our usual standard.

I am sorry we did not tell you that we were unable to repair your brand of fax machine, that we arrived so much later than you needed and that we sent you an account. I would have been annoyed if it had happened to us.

Your letter did encourage us to review our service. We are sure that it was a rare event and hope that you will continue to consider us when you need any other brands of office equipment repaired or replaced.

Thank you for taking the trouble to write to me.

Yours sincerely

Neil Jones

Neil Jones
BRANCH MANAGER
OFFICE EQUIPMENT LIMITED

Encl.: credit note for $75.86.

HERE'S OUR SIDE OF THE STORY. PLEASE PAY UP

Dear Dr Smith

INVOICE 56352

Thank you for your letter questioning our account for $75.86, but we believe it is fully justified.

Our receptionist recalls the conversation with your office manager very clearly. She remembers asking which brand of fax machine you operate and that your office manager replied, 'I don't know. Does it matter? Just fix it will you'. Your Rawhide brand is the only one we cannot service, and rare, so she decided to accept the job. I believe it was the correct decision.

We cannot provide spare parts for the Rawhide fax but our service technician made a conscientious effort to check whether he could fix your machine without replacing parts. It was soon clear that he could not and he abandoned the call so that you did not incur further cost.

Clearly, it would have been better if we had known the brand of your fax machine and had referred your office manager to another company, but we did ask.

We would appreciate prompt payment.

Yours sincerely

Neil Jones

Neil Jones
BRANCH MANAGER
OFFICE EQUIPMENT LIMITED

THANKS FOR THE BUSINESS

It's too valuable an opportunity to miss. Thank clients for choosing you. Help them to feel good about what might have been a difficult choice. It's an opportunity to build relationships. Look for ways of making it informal and personal.

Dear Mrs Jones

Thanks for choosing Smith, Smith and Smythe.

I'm delighted to welcome you as a client and I know that Sarah and her team are looking forward to working with you on the redesign of your offices.

We set ourselves very high standards of service and I want to encourage you to expect excellence from us.

Sarah will be in touch within the next few days. I hope to meet you during your next visit.

Sincerely

Peter Smith

Peter Smith Snr
CHIEF EXECUTIVE

YOU MISSED SOMETHING IMPORTANT

If your customer sends you an order or a request that's incomplete, be careful to avoid blame when you ask for clarification. Instead, treat the omission as an opportunity to enhance your business relationship.

For example, let's imagine that you sell cars to businesses and your customer has sent you an order for five cars but hasn't told you what colour she wants.

Dear Sue

ORDER FOR XL SEDANS

Thanks for the order for the five sedans. I can confirm that we can supply them with all the specifications you listed and at the prices on your order form.

Do you have any preferences for colours?

The current brochure shows the XL model in white and red on pages 5 and 6 but we can also supply it in silver, burgundy and blue.

We have XLs in all the available colours in the yard and showroom at the moment. Do call me on my direct line 9574 9597 if you would like me to locate them for you.

Once I have your decision on the colour (or colours) I can get your order under way and we should be able to deliver your XLs to each of the branches by the end of the week.

Sincerely

Peter Jones

Peter Jones
SALES MANAGER

Encl.: brochure XL and CV models.

■ EMPLOYMENT ISSUES

I RESIGN
(Internal mail)

Dear Cynthia

I have decided to resign from my position as Customer Service Manager, St Leonards Branch, from the end of the month.

I go with mixed feelings.

Steele and Company have offered me a position with some exciting challenges, but I will miss the team at Bates Brothers.

Thank you for all your support and encouragement throughout the five years I have been with the St Leonards branch.

Sincerely

Jane Smith

Jane Smith
SALES REPRESENTATIVE

SORRY YOU'RE LEAVING

(Internal mail)

Dear Jane

We will be sorry to see you go.

You have been a valuable member of our team and several of the executive staff have already commented to me that you will be difficult to replace.

You leave with our thanks and very best wishes for your new job with Steele and Company.

Regards

Cynthia Jones

Cynthia Jones
CHIEF EXECUTIVE OFFICER

OKAY, SO YOU ARE LEAVING

(Internal mail)

Dear Bill

Thank you for your letter of resignation.

I have passed your departure date on to accounts so that they can have everything ready for your final cheque on September 4.

I was sorry to read that your two years with us have been such a disappointment to you, but wish you well in your new venture in retailing.

Sincerely

Cynthia Jones

Cynthia Jones
CHIEF EXECUTIVE OFFICER

SORRY, NO JOB GOING AT THE MOMENT

Dear Paul

EMPLOYMENT ENQUIRY

Thank you for your interest in joining our sales team.

At the moment we don't have a position to offer you, but we were impressed with your CV and references and would like to keep them on file. Please call me if you would prefer to have them returned.

I should add that vacancies only come up occasionally, so it would pay to keep looking.

Good luck!

Yours sincerely

James Jones

James Jones
PERSONNEL MANAGER
RADICAL MARKETING

CONGRATULATIONS. LET'S NEGOTIATE

Dear Catherine

VACANCY FOR GRADUATE ENGINEER

We are delighted to let you know that you are our preferred candidate for the job.

The panel was impressed with your CV and your interview and we all hope we will be able to welcome you to our team once the negotiations are complete.

Please call me in the next few days so that we can arrange to negotiate the terms of employment and a salary package.

Congratulations.

Sincerely

Anthony Jones

Anthony Jones
CHIEF EXECUTIVE OFFICER
JONES JACOBSEN AND JOHNSTON

Dear Derek

VACANCY FOR GRADUATE ENGINEER

Thank you for your interest in joining our team.

The panel was impressed with your qualifications and your interview, but we have decided to offer the position to another candidate.

You might like to know that you were near the top of a list of 115 candidates — many of them with at least 10 years of relevant experience.

Best wishes in your search for your first appointment.

Sincerely

Anthony Jones

Anyhony Jones
CHIEF EXECUTIVE OFFICER
JONES JACOBSEN AND JOHNSTON

Encl.: curriculum vitae and reference.

THANKS FOR APPLYING

Dear Mr Smith

VACANCY FOR GRADUATE ENGINEER

Thank you for replying to our advertisement.

We looked through your application and curriculum vitae carefully, but have decided to offer the position to another candidate.

I wish you success in finding a position with another organisation.

Sincerely

Anthony Jones

Anthony Jones
CHIEF EXECUTIVE OFFICER
JONES JACOBSEN AND JOHNSTON

Encl.: curriculum vitae and two references.

WARNING LETTER

A warning letter should always follow some discussion in which you give your employee the opportunity to explain. You must be fair and act in good faith at each stage.

A written warning is for the record, so don't hesitate to tell the reader what he already knows. Simplicity and directness are essential.

Dear John

FORMAL WARNING

We need a written record of our discussion.

I am formally warning you that I may terminate your employment with us if you fail to complete the customer service training I have arranged for you, or you continue to be rude or discourteous to our customers.

This morning we discussed each of 10 incidents that have upset customers and you accepted that my notes on them were accurate. You also accepted that in seven of the incidents you used inappropriate language or were brusque with the customers who later complained to me.

We have appreciated your extensive knowledge of our products and your willingness to work long hours and I hope you will commit yourself to improving your relationships with customers so that you can continue to be part of the team.

Sincerely

Anthony Jones

Anthony Jones
CHIEF EXECUTIVE OFFICER
JONES JACOBSEN AND JOHNSTON

HERE'S THE JOB FOR YOU

Most people write job ads that read like public notices. It's a pity because they miss an opportunity to sell the job to a wide range of candidates and advertise the qualities and values of their organisation. Make sure you offer some benefits.

MANAGER, FIRST IMPRESSIONS

Enjoy working with people? Ready for a challenge?

We're looking for someone with a proven record in customer service.

You'll greet our customers at reception, take their calls and messages, and listen to their needs and preferences. You'll get to know them.

Here's the challenge.

It's not an ordinary receptionist role. We have extraordinarily high standards. We'll give you training, but we'll expect you to be an exceptional person. Every day.

You'll enjoy it. Not only the challenge of such a vital role, but the culture at Mason's. You'll be joining a team of positive people. They're all people *people* and fun to be around.

Ready to join the market leaders?

Contact ...

HERE'S THE JOB FOR YOU

Here's a more low-key style, but still incorporating benefits and conveying the qualities and values of the organisation. Be very specific about what you are offering and what you require.

CHEF FOR COUNTRY HOTEL

Here's the offer

A chance to produce fine cuisine for discerning customers from all over the world.
Generous days off.
Opportunities for skiing, hiking or sightseeing in one of the most scenic locations in the country.
Subsidised accommodation.

Here's what you'll need

An exemplary record in preparing fine cuisine.
Creative flair.
The ability to lead a team under pressure.
Energy and enthusiasm.
An appropriate qualification.

You'll be joining a modern hotel and a team with a reputation for excellence in food and hospitality.

Send your CV to ...

■ COLLEAGUES AND FRIENDS IN BUSINESS

We'll assume here that a telephone call or a personal visit isn't practical or that you want to provide a written record. Your letters to colleagues and friends may break more conventions. They may even be casual, depending of course on the closeness of your relationship.

THANK YOU

Be specific about what you appreciated. If you can, provide some evidence of its effect or some element of 'news'.

Dear Peta

Thanks for all the help with the marketing plan. You did a wonderful job. It looks stunning.

I sent the plan to the directors yesterday and a couple of them have already mentioned how impressed they are with the layout and especially your graphs. Mr Williams asked about your background.

Thanks too for your enthusiasm, especially when the pressure was on.

I really enjoyed working with you.

Regards

Paula

CONDOLENCES

Feelings are paramount. Don't hesitate to express them, but strive for genuine emotional support rather than either the gushiness or aloofness that comes with clichés. The detail will depend on the closeness of your relationship, but if it's a death, aim to make your initial contact short.

Dear Paul

I am thinking of you.

It was a dreadful shock to hear of Lynda's death and I've found it impossible to concentrate on anything else this morning. The office is very subdued. We are all preoccupied with the news of the accident and feelings of support for you and your family.

Please don't feel under any additional pressure from work. We've cleared your appointments and Sandra has put your key accounts in a holding pattern.

Please let me know if there's anything we can do.

Regards

Peter Jones

■ MISCELLANEOUS

THANKS. YOU DID WELL

Get personal, with appropriate informality. Lofty, cold, impersonal writing will make your thanks seem grudging. Tell your reader how much you and others appreciated the work. Be specific (that's direct) in your praise. Include any reservations so that it's not gushy, but if you genuinely intend to praise, allow for the fact that for many people reservations or criticism often carry more weight than congratulations. Include the next step or some element of 'news'.

Dear Graham

I read your report last night and I'm impressed.

I'm not totally convinced about the staffing levels you're recommending, but you've put together a carefully reasoned report with an admirable range of original, practical ideas that will get all of us thinking.

Peter was in this morning. He shares my enthusiasm for your report (and even agrees with you about the staffing).

We need some action before the end of the month. Could you come to Head Office sometime next week for a meeting with our senior team?

Congratulations. It's a valuable contribution.

Regards

Henry Smith

Henry Smith
CHIEF EXECUTIVE

PLEASE REPLY

Sometimes, when you want your readers to reply, there's very little in it for them. The challenge is to find a benefit, perhaps as simple as feeling good about helping. You should also make your letter informal and personal. Tell them how easy it will be to respond.

Dear Mrs Williams

A CHANCE TO HAVE YOUR SAY

Here's a chance to express some frank opinions, and get results.

Although we haven't done business together so far, we'd be grateful if you could take a few minutes to complete the questionnaire. We don't need names but we would value your comments on the service, décor, facilities and catering of the conference venues you've used.

You'll be helping to lift the standards of most of the venues in this city.

Let me explain that.

You'll be helping us discover what people who hold conferences value most. It's such a competitive business that we can be sure that the other venues will match the changes we make, perhaps within a few months. Even if you never do business with us, you'll benefit. (Of course we'd like to talk to you about being a client too, but that's a separate issue.)

Thanks in anticipation.

Sincerely

Jocelyn Jones

Jocelyn Jones
MARKETING MANAGER
OVATION CONFERENCES

I'D LIKE TO MAKE AN APPOINTMENT

This kind of letter works well for salespeople wanting to set up appointments, but it's suitable for anyone who wants to introduce an idea and encourage the reader to consider a meeting.

The words 'I plan to call you soon' will almost ensure that your reader reads it all. Add some possible benefits but don't tell the reader what would be good for them.

Dear Mrs Jones

SOLUTIONS FOR HR MANAGERS

I plan to call you soon and thought you might appreciate some background first.

Efficient Software distributes software designed to make life easier for human resource managers. We are based here in St Leonards.

I would appreciate a few minutes on the telephone to explore whether it would be worth meeting to look at how we might help you.

I'd need to do some listening before I could suggest anything specific, but there's a wide range of possibilities. Most of our clients particularly appreciate having software especially designed by people with real management experience. Many value our payroll software because it saves them the cost and hassle of contracting out payroll management. Others enjoy the convenience of in-house computer training programs.

I'll be in touch in the next few days.

Sincerely

Rachel Smith

Rachel Smith
SALES REPRESENTATIVE
EFFICIENT SOFTWARE

THANKS FOR THE MEETING

You might write one of these letters as a courtesy when you are particularly grateful for the opportunity to meet. Keep it simple and informal. Try to avoid clichés and see if you can find something new to mention — perhaps a development since the discussion or some additional information that extends the discussion or illustrates how useful it was.

Dear Jennifer

I appreciated your time on Tuesday, especially in such a busy week.

Your thoughts on the 'glass ceiling' issue have been especially useful and I have decided to put them into a separate article to accompany the main feature. Unless you have any objection, we'd like to use the photograph we took last year for the story about public speaking.

I've been talking to several of my women colleagues about the key points you made. One discussion became particularly animated and I'm sure there'll be many more around the country once the next edition goes out.

Many thanks.

Sincerely

Patsy Jones

Patsy Jones
STAFF WRITER
WOMEN IN BUSINESS

THANKS FOR THE SALES MEETING

Salespeople should write more of them. Even if you leave your card, it's too easy for the prospective client to forget you and the meeting. Use the letter or email to advance the relationship. You should always give yourself a task at the end of meetings with prospective clients and you can refer to the brochure, report or enquiry you promised.

Dear Mr Williams

Thanks for the opportunity to meet on Friday. I appreciated the time that you put into our discussion and found your experience with the many brands on the market particularly useful.

I have been following up the concerns you had about how the heating elements might perform in heavy frosts and our engineers tell me that the elements for the X25 model are designed to operate in temperatures down to minus 30 degrees Celsius.

We were lucky with the manual for the 1992 models. There were only a few left. You'll find the exploded diagram of the crankshaft components on page 28.

The brochure I promised has the P24 and ZL4 models. I'd like to contact you so that we can discuss which would be most appropriate for the trial you suggested.

Thanks again.

Sincerely

James Smythe

James Smythe
SALES REPRESENTATIVE
GLOBAL TRANSPORT SOLUTIONS

Encl.: 1992 manual, brochures for P24 and ZL4.

■ LAST WORD

Commit yourself to becoming an effective communicator. All it takes is focus and practice.

There's nothing surprising or academic about effective writing. Make a commitment to improving not only your writing, but your communication generally. Everyday conversation gives us opportunities to develop our skills.

Work on being more audience-centred and making your conversations simpler. Use more active language, be more direct and show the relevance of your topic to people, especially your readers and audiences. The golden rule of all communication and the five keys are enough to make you an effective communicator. With practice, they will become a way of life.

Use the editing system so that you not only revise your work more efficiently, but become more familiar with the five keys. Before long, there'll be much less editing to do.

Become a critic. When you sense that any writing isn't working, be specific. Could it be simpler, more informal, direct, active or personal?

If you are a fluent speaker of English you have an extraordinary skill. All you have to do is to use it in your writing in a focused way. The five keys to effective writing give you that focus.

Don't be put off by past disappointments or criticism. I've seen people who thought they had no potential become very competent business writers. All they needed was to release themselves from the burden of the imagined formal rules of business English and concentrate on communication.

Persuade your colleagues to change too. It's not difficult. I've found that even people who believe that the stuffy clichés give their writing authority or credibility will willingly acknowledge the improvement when you show them a completed, reworked text. If you can change the in-house style to the five keys, you'll be able to edit each other's work without having to do major rewrites that take unnecessary time and demoralise writers.

Look for opportunities in your writing, presentations and conversations to grab your audience's attention and hold it. Look for ways to improve the flow and rhythm, to surprise, to build rapport by acknowledging shared understanding. If you can also use contrasts and the Rule of Three regularly and appropriately, you're a graduate of the master class.

We all need to persuade, and it's in everyone's interests that we learn how to persuade effectively. As we've seen, we need to do much more than simply provide what we believe to be relevant facts. The facts must be relevant to the audience's decision making. Be clear about your proposal, then take some time to ask yourself why your audience would not accept it. Pre-empt those objections, paint pictures and acknowledge feelings.

See writing as a skill you can develop throughout your life. Above all, enjoy the richness of your language.

INDEX

NOTES

NOTES